Getting Into and Surviving College

LEARNING
HOW TO
LEARN

When You Have a Learning Disability

Revised Edition

★ ★ ★ ★ ★

Joyanne Cobb

Child & Family Press   Washington, D.C.

Child & Family Press is an imprint of the Child Welfare League of America. The Child Welfare League of America is the nation's oldest and largest membership-based child welfare organization. We are committed to engaging people everywhere in promoting the well-being of children, youth, and their families, and protecting every child from harm.

CHILD WELFARE LEAGUE OF AMERICA, INC.
HEADQUARTERS
440 First Street, NW, Third Floor, Washington, DC 20001-2085
E-mail: books@cwla.org

CURRENT PRINTING (last digit)
10 9 8 7 6 5 4 3 2 1

Cover design by Meredith Simpson
Text design by Pen & Palette

Printed in the United States of America
ISBN # 0-87868-878-1

Library of Congress Cataloging-in-Publication Data

Cobb, Joyanne.
   Learning how to learn : getting into and surviving college when you
have a learning disability / Joyanne Cobb.– Rev. ed.
       p. cm.
Includes bibliographical references.
   ISBN 0-87868-878-1 (alk. paper)
   1. Learning disabled youth–Education (Higher)–United States. 2.
Universities and colleges–United States–Admission. I. Title.
   LC4818.38.C62 2003
   371.92'6–dc21
                                      2002156472

CONTENTS

ACKNOWLEDGMENTS

As we begin the second printing of this book, I look back on the past year and the many people I have spoken to—both by email and in person—about what the book has meant to them. It is those people that have helped me persevere in this endeavor and believe that another edition of this book will continue to do good work. There are some additions and changes I think that you will find very helpful.

First and foremost, I would like to express my deepest gratitude to Barbara Seaman, a now-retired English professor, without whom this book would not have happened. She not only helped me develop the overall vision of this book, but devoted hours of assistance with research, editing, and revisions. More than that, she believed in me when I did not believe in myself, made me fight the system and appeal a graduate school entrance decision, and was a mother to me in many ways. Her support and inspiration has and always will carry me through the tough times.

Cathy Corder came to my rescue as a tutor in college and then realized I had a wealth of information that I should share with the world in the form of this book. I will never forget her tireless hours of work with me.

Christy Willis of the George Washington University was a savior to me and many other students at the Disabled Student Service office. She is still there today.

Erica Lovelace of the Virginia Department of Rehabilitation Services implemented a great and thorough plan for me.

My dear friend from college, Djuana Parmely, now a law student, has allowed me to tell her story when talking to youth with mobility obstacles.

I have been lucky enough to know people who have supported me in many ways and never asked for anything in return. You have all been guiding lights at different times in my life.

A special thanks goes to my family: My mother, for instilling in me that as a woman I can be anything I want to be; my father, who always tells me he is proud of who I have become; my brothers and sisters, who have understood that due to the book I just do not have as much time to spend with them as I would like; and to my two nephews, both with disabilities of their own, who remind me every day why a book such as this one is necessary.

And finally, a big thank you goes to the Child Welfare League of America for taking a chance on an unknown author, and particularly to Tegan Culler, Peggy Tierney, and Francine Bennett for their thoughtful editing and book marketing. Your efforts here will continue to make a difference for many learning disabled persons.

—*Joyanne Cobb*

Introduction

THE INVISIBLE DISABILITY

So you want to go to college—but you have a learning disability. I also struggled through high school with a learning disability, and my counselors were convinced that I should just prepare for a career at some fast-food outlet. But I decided that I deserved better. I got into college and got my undergraduate degree. I finished graduate school and earned a master's degree—and I also learned a lot about how learning disabled students like you and me can succeed in college.

If you are learning disabled, you are a person who learns differently. Sure, you have a disability, in the sense that you receive and process information differently—so that you can't learn in the traditional ways that your peers do. You may have visual sequencing problems that cause you to have trouble seeing things in correct order. You may have visual discrimination problems and can't see the difference between two similar objects, letters, or numbers. Or maybe you have a form of a processing disorder called dyslexia, which causes you to see letters, syllables, words, and even numbers reversed or just out of order. Speech and language disorders are another form of a learning disability. These include articulation disorder, which affects your ability to control speech rate; expressive language disorder, which is a problem expressing yourself in speech; and receptive language disorder, which is trouble understanding certain aspects of speech.

These are just some of the reasons why you learn differently, and that puts you at a disadvantage. When you start the race 50 yards behind the other runners, you can't be expected to finish at the same time everyone else does.

One of the most painful things about having a learning disability is that it is very difficult for people to understand. Just as with racism and bigotry, that which we do not understand we treat differently—and sometimes with more than a little animosity. I believe this lack of understanding is the most difficult thing for people with learning disabilities and for their families to deal with.

I never realized how painful this invisible disability was for me until one night in October 1990. I had been asked to participate on a panel during Disability Awareness Week at George Washington University, where I was an undergraduate. On the panel were other people with various disabilities. A male student and I represented the learning disabled population.

The format was for each person on the panel to tell our "stories," followed by a question-and-answer period. I was doing fine until someone in the audience asked me, "What is the hardest thing about having a disability that you cannot see? I can see that she is in a wheelchair and he is blind, but how do people react to someone who looks fine but claims to be disabled? I mean, you look fine to me."

For a long time there was silence. I remember staring at the sign language interpreter as she waited patiently for me to respond. At that point, I could feel the tears welling up in my eyes and my face starting to burn. I began to say, "You know, it is so hard to ask for help when people think that you don't need it or don't understand why you need it," but I couldn't get all this out in one fell swoop. I began to cry. I kept saying, "Wait a minute," as I tried to collect myself and muster what little dignity I had left to finish what I was trying to say. To tell you the truth, I don't remember if I ever got the whole statement out, but I think about 70 people understood something about a learning disability that night.

Going to college may be more difficult for someone who is learning disabled, but I know from experience that it can be done. Your decision to go to college is the right one, because it is what you want to do, and that is all the justification you need.

This guide is designed to help you reach your goals. In a nutshell, this book will address

✎ knowing your rights under the Americans with Disabilities Act of 1990 (ADA),

✎ preparing for college by thinking about issues and concerns in high school,

✎ getting the proper documentation of your learning disability to ensure you get services you need,

✎ taking the SAT and the ACT,

✎ researching schools with services for the learning disabled,

✎ asking the questions that will help you choose the college or university that is right for you,

✎ making your college life easier with assistive technology (computer programs and other instruments),

✎ and adapting my own tips for getting into and surviving college with a learning disability.

Along the way I have shared my own experiences, so you can understand the challenges you will be meeting. I hope you will find some useful suggestions in the stories I have to tell.

You need to know that you can go to college and succeed. I am proof of that, though I made some mistakes along the way. My hope is that this guide will help you avoid making the same mistakes that I did. You may be able to get your bachelor's degree in four or five years—instead of seven years, like me. But do keep in mind that, although it may take you longer than other people, **it can be done!**

Chapter 1

THE AMERICANS WITH DISABILITIES ACT

Having a learning disability means, quite simply, that you have a disability. Educators, psychological professionals, medical professionals, and even learning disabled persons like you often do not make this connection. This missed connection is why persons with learning disabilities often do not access and utilize the legislation that exists to protect their right to reasonable accommodations.

KNOW THE LAW

All civil rights laws that concern persons with disabilities, from the Rehabilitation Act of 1973 to the Americans with Disabilities Act of 1990 (ADA), do recognize individuals with learning disabilities. This means that you are entitled to the same unique civil rights protections given to persons with other types of disabilities. Your coverage under this Act is relevant to your college education.

Under the ADA, the term "disability" means a physical or mental impairment that substantially limits a person in a major life activity. Persons with a learning disability are covered here because a major life function, (i.e., learning) is substantially limited or impaired. In an educational setting, however, you must meet or exceed the standards of the program you are entering. The law states that a qualified individual with a disability is someone who, with or without reasonable accommodations, can meet the criteria for entry into the educational program. Although they are required to provide "reasonable accommodation" for your disability once you are admitted, colleges do not have to change their educational standards for admittance in order to accommodate you. You must first meet their criteria for admittance before gaining access to these civil rights.

Under the ADA, "reasonable accommodation" may include auxiliary aids and services a learning disabled person may require. Auxiliary aids and services include qualified interpreters or other effective methods of making aurally delivered materials available, qualified readers, taped texts, acquisition or modified equipment or devices, and other similar services and actions. These "reasonable accommodations" are the things that allow you as a student to achieve your goals.

The college will require professional documentation of your learning disability prior to providing accommodations. Part of understanding your rights under the Americans With Disabilities Act (ADA) is understanding the federal definition of a learning disability. Under federal law, certain criteria must exist for a child to be eligible for special education services due to a specific learning disability. If you have met these requirements, then chances are you will be eligible for accommodations at the college and university level. These requirements are listed in Chapter 3.

It will be up to you to disclose your disability and to decide when to do so. Disability laws forbid employers or educational institutions from asking if a person has a disability. This means it is up to you to self-disclose in order to be guaranteed protection under the law. Do not wait to disclose after you are in trouble in a class. This will create even more stress, and it may be too late for the college help you.

SELF-ADVOCACY

An essential part of your success is your ability to advocate for yourself. Not that you should set up picket lines and start a coalition, but you should learn how to ask for what you need. Keep in mind that it is your **right** to be accommodated. However, if you don't ask for those accommodations, you won't get them. As I have already mentioned, learning disabilities are invisible. That means that the average Joe is not going to be able to see what you need.

To advocate for yourself means to speak up and speak to the right people. If your professors are not familiar with learning disabilities, then use the opportunity to educate them. Talk about your experiences with LD peers in your support and resources groups. You are your own greatest advocate, and just as you have had to learn how to learn, you will have to self-advocate to survive in college.

Some people think that the "LD" should stand for "Learning Differently," not "Learning Disabled." You're right to refer to yourself as someone who learns differently. But if we only say that we are people who learn **differently**, then we are also saying that we are not **disabled**. In that case, legislation on accommodations for the disabled would no longer apply to us. Consequently, when you describe yourself as someone who learns differently, you're perfectly right. But when you are fighting for accommodations in a traditional academic arena, you should refer to yourself as "learning disabled."

RESOURCES

Finally, know the law. Understanding the ADA is important because it entitles you to the accommodations that you deserve. I have found in my career and in life that most issues can be worked out with educated discussion, but many times you have to do the educating—and it is OK to get help with this. Here are some toll-free numbers you can use to find out about what the ADA provides for a person with a learning disability:

- ✎ **The ADA Information Line** can answer your questions about the law, send you free material, and advise you on how to file an ADA complaint. Voice: 800/514-0301; TDD: 800/514-0383.

- ✎ **The ADA Information Center for the Mid-Atlantic region** can provide you with the same general information. 800/949-4232.

- ✎ **Department of Justice Information Line** can give you information about the **Rehabilitation Act (Section 504),** another law that protects your rights, and can advise you about filing a complaint on violations other than educational ones. 800/514-0301.

✎ **Department of Education, Office of Civil Rights** not only answers questions about **Section 504** but also provides advice on how to file a **Section 504** complaint on education-related issues. 800/421-3481

✎ **The National Center for Law and Learning Disabilities (NCLLD)** is a nonprofit education and advocacy organization providing legal information and resources for the learning disabled. 301/469-8308.

To make the law work for you, however, you must be able to document your disability and know what accommodations you need. Find out about your legal rights; they are an essential part of your educational plan.

PART ONE

GETTING INTO COLLEGE

Classroom 101

Chapter 2

PREPARING FOR COLLEGE

I cannot emphasize enough that this journey you are embarking on, this path of higher education, will be a constant process of learning how to learn. For you to accomplish your goal—obtaining a college degree—you will need to make many preparations. It's a process that should begin when you start high school. It is a long process, but with the right planning and assistance, you can do it.

Let me begin by telling you just a little about my experience in high school, before I even started thinking about going to college. At that time, I didn't believe I had the ability to make my own decisions about anything related to school. I was led to believe that I was lacking something, and therefore, deciding what classes I was going to take was something I couldn't possibly do right.

I had a counselor who saw that I could not succeed in the classroom (my grades were proof of that), so I was signed up for classes like "Leadership," which was an invaluable experience and probably helped my self-esteem somewhat. But I was registered for a lot of study hall, too. Because I failed most of the science and math courses I took, I had little to show that I could succeed in the classroom—that I could learn.

I had done a science project in which I designed my own methods to present a problem and conducted experiments to examine that problem. My project was on acid rain, and I presented it to the International Science and Engineering Fair for four consecutive years. I did it at my own pace and was able to present it orally in competitions, instead of on paper or in an exam format. This option was ideal for me, as someone who learns differently, since I could not pass a chemistry class to save my life and did a mediocre job in biology courses.

Although I felt confident about my project, after I returned to the classroom I was unable to comprehend the same information I had used in my experiment, because I didn't understand the way it was presented. While other students with good science projects were being offered scholarships to colleges, I was left behind with a great project but failing grades. When other students would ask me where I was going to college, I wanted so much to be like them that I would lie and say, "Oh, I got offers, too, but I don't know where I'll be going."

Then, the summer before my senior year in high school, I was given a scholarship to a summer college science program, with the option of attending that college after graduation. There I worked with a college professor on my research and science project, did well, and was even chosen to return the next year and present it at a junior science symposium. But another part of that program was to take classes—and pass them. Again, the roadblocks went up. Of all the students who made presentations, I was the only one with no plans to attend college after graduation. I struggled with this bleak prospect for a long time. Many people would see me with my science project and then expect me to reproduce it successfully on paper or in the classroom. They just automatically thought that I'd be going to a great college or university and have all my ducks in a row. But the truth was, my ducks were drowning, and I really did not have a plan to save them.

I started my uphill battle at the University of Florida by failing those classes, then going to a community college in my hometown and failing there. I dealt with all this failure by making bad choices about drugs and alcohol. Through it all, though, I knew I had to figure out what I needed to reach my potential— potential I knew I had. I had to learn how to learn all over again. With each failure and each school, I learned something. It took me seven years to get my bachelor's degree, but I did it. Along the way I found out more and more things about what would make learning easier for me. Eventually I found a community college that provided an environment that allowed me to learn, and then I transferred to one of the best universities in the country with superb services for learning disabled students, The George Washington University. I hope that this book and the account of my journey makes yours an easier one.

SCHEDULING: THE FIRST STEP

So how can you avoid similar roadblocks? The first important step you should take to prepare for college is to have a "hands-on" experience with your high school class schedule. You should allow your counselor to help, but you must know your own capabilities, too. You probably have had to "learn how to learn" all your life, so your input into deciding which classes to take will be invaluable as you journey toward your college degree.

As I said before, you know what you can do, so you are the best judge of the workload you can carry each semester. You should certainly take some courses in subjects that you will enjoy, but don't let a counselor or a teacher tell you that these are the **only** ones that you can do well in. And when you are making your schedule, be sure to consider participation in extracurricular activities.

My Experience: I did well in extracurricular activities, but I didn't have good grades. Then, too, my time management skills were poor. Because I succeeded in activities outside the classroom, I wanted to do more of them. As a result, I spent so little time on the classwork that I failed miserably. On the other hand, my success in extracurricular activities gave me good memories of high school. I did well on the tennis court, in a speech tournament, and on the stage. Without these activities, I probably would have felt like a complete failure and may not have had the little confidence I did. I recommend participation in extracurricular activities, but participate with caution. Limit yourself. Be sure to make the extra time you need to put into that difficult class. You need to feel success and accomplishment outside the classroom, but don't overdo it to the point that you jeopardize your success in the classroom.

INDIVIDUAL EDUCATION PLAN

Some of you may have had the opportunity to make choices for yourself in the writing of your Individual Education Plan (IEP). Although student involvement in IEPs is now a recommended policy, it may not occur regularly in all schools. I was not involved in this process and did not know that I should have been. Had I been involved, I could have taken a first step toward self-empowerment, and perhaps my journey through college wouldn't have been such a long one. So my advice is to be involved in this process. It is best for you in the long run, as it will help you to realize your challenges and strengths.

Transition Planning

Transition is the passage from one stage of development to another. In this context, transition refers to the passage of the learning disabled youth from high school to post-secondary education, and that transition requires preparation. For young adults who have learning disabilities, this transition stage is critical to the rest of their lives.

The Individuals with Disabilities Education Act (IDEA), passed in 1990, stipulates that all students who receive services under IDEA must have transition planning beginning at age 14. The Transition Plan is part of the IEP. This is a coordinated set of activities that are outcome orientated and based on the needs of the student. The Transition Plan should promote movement toward certain stated goals. For our purposes here, this plan should reflect your goal of obtaining a postsecondary education.

The professionals who gather once a year for your Individualized Education Plan should also be part of your transition planning. Your transition team should also include any professional or service provider who has been involved in your education.

The best thing that you can do as the student receiving the transition planning services is be involved. This is your future, not the future of the others involved. If you have a certain postsecondary institution in mind, then you need to make sure your Transition Plan is geared toward accomplishing what you need to get into that college or university.

The transition plan should include:

✎ Your identified interests

✎ Your identified needs

✎ Your identified postschool outcomes

✎ A coordinated set of activities that will assist you in reaching these outcomes

✎ Self-advocacy preparation

✎ Linkages to postsecondary education and training needs

✎ Linkages to adult support service needs

This Transition Plan will be the map you need to get you on your way to the postsecondary education you have been dreaming about.

FOREIGN LANGUAGES

For many learning disabled people, learning a foreign language is a major roadblock. Since this is a requirement in many high schools and colleges, learning disabled students face a seemingly insurmountable barrier. Therefore, scheduling a foreign language course is something to consider carefully. Begin by finding out if your high school requires a foreign language for graduation and whether the colleges you are considering require it.

As a learning disabled person, you need to consider many factors in your decision to study a foreign language: the instructor, the pace at which the class is taught, and the experiences you have had with studying a foreign language, if any. You will be more likely to succeed with a language that uses a familiar alphabet. If you have had difficulty with one language, try a new one. In addition to these considerations, you should also find out about your peers in the course. If most of the other students have no experience in this language, you may find yourself (maybe for the first time) at the same starting point as other students.

My Experience: My first attempt to learn a foreign language was with Spanish. I started out well enough, but only seemed to get worse as the class moved on, and I began to repeat my frustrating experiences trying to learn to write in English. The next disaster was Latin. (Yes, I even flunked Latin.) That experience was particularly frustrating, because I had a very difficult time understanding the differences between words, whether I heard them or read them. It's no surprise that when I had the choice, I opted to take a foreign culture course in college.

Some teachers of foreign languages are reassessing their thinking about dyslexic learners, and some may be able to modify their courses to accommodate your needs. For example, many people with learning disabilities can learn a foreign language auditorily by using cassette tapes or by using a computer program that allows them to learn by visual cues. A software program, <u>Climbing with Phonics</u>, is now available for those with "phonemic awareness" problems.

If your learning disability prevents you from learning a foreign language, however, check to see if you have the option to take a foreign culture course or if you can substitute any other class. Finally, if you have no other option, find out if you can have the foreign language requirement waived. A list of publications and electronic sources on learning disabilities and foreign languages appears at the end of this chapter.

To sum up, some of the challenges you may face in preparing for college involve becoming active in your class scheduling and taking courses that may be required by colleges or universities, such as foreign languages. With a little planning and some work, however, you can meet these challenges.

PRINT RESOURCES ON LEARNING DISABILITIES AND ADD/ADHD

Bell, N. (1991). <u>Visualizing and verbalizing</u> (2nd ed.). Paso Robles, CA: Academy of Reading Publications.

Clark, D.B. & Uhrey, J.K. (1995). <u>Dyslexia: Theory & practice of remedial instruction</u>. (2nd ed.). Baltimore: York Press.

Franklin, L., Hodge, M.E., & Sasscer, M.F. (1997). Improving retention with strategy-based instruction. The Journal of the Virginia Community Colleges, 1(2).

PRINT RESOURCES ON LEARNING DISABILITIES AND FOREIGN LANGUAGES

Bacon, S.M. (1996). Choices in postsecondary foreign language programs. In B. H. Wing (Ed.), Foreign languages for all: Challenges and choices (pp. 91–114). Lincolnwood, IL: National Textbook Company.

Otto, S. K., & Pusak, J. P. (1996). Technological choices to meet the challenges. In B. H. Wing (Ed.), Foreign languages for all: Challenges and choices (pp. 141–186). Lincolnwood, IL: National Textbook Company.

Sparks, R., & Ganschow, L. (1993). The impact of native language learning problems on foreign language learning: Case study illustrations of the linguistic coding deficit hypothesis. The Modern Language Journal, 77, 58–74.

Sparks, R., Ganschow, L., Pohlman, J., Skinner, S., & Artzer, M. (1992). The effect of multisensory structured language instruction on native language and foreign language aptitude skills of at-risk foreign language learners. Annals of Dyslexia, 42, 25–53.

ONLINE RESOURCES ON LEARNING DISABILITIES AND FOREIGN LANGUAGES

The Coordinated Campaign for Learning Disabilities. (1997). Commonly asked questions about learning disabilities. Online: www. ldonline.org/

Dartmouth College. (1997). Academic success video series for college students. Online: www.dartmouth.edu/admin/acskills/

Schwartz, R. L. (1997). Learning disabilities and foreign language learning: A painful collision. Online: www.ldonline.org/ld_indepth/foreign_lang/painful_collision.html.

Sedita, J. (1996). A call for more study skills: Instruction. Online: www.ldonline.org/

Chapter 3

DOCUMENTING YOUR LEARNING DISABILITY

Obtaining documentation of your learning disability can be a frustrating issue. This proof of your disability is very important to your college career, however. You will need official documentation of your learning disability to obtain accommodations when you take standardized tests such as the PSAT, SAT, or ACT. Furthermore, the college you are entering will request proof of your learning disability diagnosis for you to use its services for disabled students or its learning disability program or learning center.

IF YOU HAVE ALREADY BEEN TESTED

Many learning disabled people are diagnosed in high school, usually through the request of a school official such as a teacher, a learning disability specialist, a special education teacher, or a parent. Of course, parental permission is always required for a student to be tested. A trained psychologist or a reading or learning specialist usually administers the test.

Even if you have been tested, it is always wise to call the colleges or universities to which you are applying to find out exactly what they require in terms of documentation. The documentation that you provide to colleges can be **no more than three years old.**

✎ If you were tested in a public school system, the tests that you were given were probably the bare minimum required to qualify you for services in your school district. Therefore, you may find that your college's Office for Disabled Student Services requires additional tests for you to qualify for the services they offer.

✎ If you were tested by a private psychologist, your parents probably paid for it, and it's likely that you got a battery of the latest LD diagnostic tests. These tests should be sufficient evidence of your disability for just about any college. Nevertheless, you must still check with the office for disabled student services or the learning center at your college to make sure that you have the documentation they require.

✎ Public school systems sometimes send students to a specialist from outside the system to be tested. If your high school referred you to an outside specialist, the school paid for this testing. Schools often use independent contractors if they don't have a psychologist on staff.

IF YOU HAVE NEVER BEEN TESTED

A few different avenues are available for testing if you are ready to enter college but don't have documentation of your learning disability. First, find out from the colleges or universities to which you are applying exactly what you will need. Local agencies in your area may be able either to perform the tests or refer you to diagnosticians. To find the appropriate agencies, check your local telephone book for adult education, adult literacy programs, or literacy councils.

Here are some other places that may help you with testing and diagnosis:

✎ The International Dyslexia Association
(formerly the Orton Dyslexia Society)
8600 LaSalle Road
Chester Building, Suite 382
Baltimore, MD 21286-2044
410/296-0232
800/222-3123
Fax:410/321-5069
www.interdys.org

There are local chapters nationwide; you can get listings from the main office.

✎ Your state or local vocational rehabilitation agency

✎ Special education programs or study skills classes and reading centers at local colleges

✎ The Disabled Students Services office at your local college or university

✎ Learning Disabilities Association of America

> 4156 Library Road
> Pittsburgh, PA 15234
> 412/341-1515
> Fax: 412/344-0224
> www.ldanatl.org

✎ Local adult education centers or career centers

✎ Local psychologists listed in the yellow pages

Be sure to ask any relevant questions before you are tested. Remember to include the following crucial points:

✎ What is the cost of the testing?

My Experience: I found out that to receive services, I needed additional testing—to the tune of $1,500!

✎ Will my insurance cover the cost of these tests?

✎ Can I work out a payment plan if I am uninsured or if my insurance will not cover these tests?

✎ Will I get a written report of the diagnosis, results, evaluation, and recommendations?

TYPES OF TESTS

No matter what the orientation of your disability is, experts generally agree that the identification of the learning disability requires a variety of tests and supplementary observations and procedures. If you were given a thorough battery of tests as a child, those results are still significant, especially if they diagnosed your specific learning disability. You will probably need additional testing, however. To familiarize yourself with some of these methods so you won't be totally in the dark when calling a college's disabled students services office or a learning center, I have summarized some of the most widely used tests or screening techniques below. They are divided into several categories (Aptitude/Cognitive, Language, Academic/Achievement tests and Specific Assessments of Learning Disabilities/Information Processing.

You never outgrow the learning disability. Under the ADA, the learning disability is life-long. But even though the learning disability will continue, the severity of the condition may change over a period of time. Therefore, if you were tested as child and the results revealed your deficiencies and diagnosis, you will still need to have updated testing and assessments done, particularly assessments used for adults. It is important that these assessments be no more than three years old.

COMMON ASSESSMENTS AND TESTS

Aptitude/Cognitive Ability

The Wechsler Adult Intelligence Scale-Revised (WAIS-R). This is a very common test. You may have been administered the children's version as a child. Although it is called an intelligence test, do not let this intimidate you. These tests are used in almost any screening process, and the intelligence quotient (IQ) helps to differentiate between mental retardation and learning disabilities. The scales also provide qualitative information about specific deficiencies in perception and recall of visual patterns, motor difficulties in copying forms, limitations in short-term memory, inability to handle abstract concepts, and many types of language deficiencies. If you are being screened for a learning disability, you will probably have to take additional tests.

If you were tested as a child, then you were probably given a version of this test known as the WISC-III. You may even have taken the preschool version of this test before you were six years old. But if you were tested in high school (after the age of 16), then you were given the WAIS-R. If you were given the WISC-III, then your college will probably ask you to get tested again. This is probably a good idea, because the WAIS-R will give you a better understanding of your areas of weakness. Knowing your "problem areas" (what you struggle with most) is very helpful when you are preparing to enter college and when you are deciding on the classes you will take during your first semester.

Parts of the test will probably be difficult for you. The scales were developed without the learning disabled in mind, and are designed more for those who learn through traditional methods. In reality, if the goal is to get an accurate measure of intelligence, this test is not fair to people with learning disabilities. Someone with a learning disability may need paper and pencil to figure out the arithmetic word problems—which are presented orally—but this test does not allow for the test-taker to use pencil and paper. No visual cues will be provided. This test is only one of many that should be used for diagnosing learning disabilities, however.

Stanford-Binet Intelligence Scale (4th ed.). This is another "intelligence" scale that is used as an alternative to the Wechsler, so it is not likely that a battery screening will have both the Stanford-Binet and the Wechsler. The Wechsler is used more widely.

The Kaufman Adolescent and Adult Intelligence Test. This is a multi-subtest battery that covers the age range from 11 years to 85 years. It is based on a model of fluid and crystallized intelligence scales. The crystallized scales measure your ability to solve problems using knowledge. The scales are as follows: Auditory Comprehension, Double Meanings, and Definitions. The fluid scales scale your ability to solve novel problems. The scales are as follows: Rebus Learning, Mystery Codes, and Logical Steps. There is also an expanded battery that includes Memory Block design, Famous Faces, Rebus Delayed Recall, and Auditory Delayed Recall.

The Woodcock-Johnson Psychoeducational Battery – Revised: Tests of Cognitive Ability. This is used as part of a thorough battery of assessments in order to diagnose a learning disability. These are often found to be used by school psychologists when updating testing for the purpose of the IEP. You may find that you have taken these before. Both of these are widely accepted for the purpose of documentation of a learning disability.

Language Tests

<u>Test of Adolescent and Adult Language—Third Edition</u>. This is an assessment of receptive and expressive language skills. It will measure listening, speaking, reading, and writing skills.

<u>Test of Written Language—3 (TOWL-3)</u>. This is an assessment of written language skills. It contains essay analysis and traditional formats to assess aspects of written language. It has easy items and is designed to be user friendly for persons with writing disabilities.

Academic/Achievement Tests

<u>Scholastic Abilities Test For Adults (SATA)</u>.

<u>Stanford Test of Academic Skills (TASK)</u>.

<u>Woodcock-Johnson Psychoeducational Battery – Revised: Test of Achievement</u>.

<u>Wechsler Individual Achievement Test (WIAT)</u>.

All of these tests assess academic achievement. They all look at specific areas of learning. These tests also assess visual and auditory learning. In most cases, your testing professional will administer only one of these tests.

Specific Assessments for Learning Disabilities/ Information Processing

<u>Nelson-Denny Reading Skills Test</u>.

<u>Stanford Diagnostic Mathematics Test</u>.

<u>Woodcock Reading Mastery Test—Revised</u>.

<u>Detroit Test of Learning Aptitude—Adult (DTLA-A)</u>. The tests listed above look at specific mental abilities. They are designed to identify students who need special help, to document specific areas of strength or weakness, and to monitor how effective accommodation and remedial efforts will be to improve performance. Your testing professional may administer more than one of these during your assessment.

It is important to note that your examiner will not use all of the assessments mentioned in the preceding section. This is only meant to provide you with an overview of the basics as far as what kind of evaluations are out there. Do not be afraid of them, and ask questions as often as you need to.

Testing professionals may use any number of less formal screening techniques. One of these is an Informal Reading Inventory. The examiner will ask the student to read passages silently or aloud, and listen as passages are read to him or her. If the student is reading out loud, the examiner will listen for any miscues or mistakes. Following the reading of each passage is a comprehension check, which may include questions about vocabulary, facts, main ideas, inferences, and sequences.

Keep in mind that it is your right to know the results of any test that is administered to you. Tell the test administrator that you expect a consultation afterward. Some school districts and testing facilities require that your parent or legal guardian be present at such a consultation if you are under 18 years of age, but remember that you have a right to be there as well.

Also, be sure that the person interpreting your tests is familiar with learning disabilities in your age range—child, adolescent, or adult. The people who can interpret your results are psychologists, rehabilitation counselors, learning and reading specialists, and LD specialists. Where and in what situation you are tested will determine whether or not you will have one, some, or all of the professionals listed above involved in the evaluation and interpretation of your tests. The term "learning disability" is defined as a significant gap between a person's intelligence and the skills the person has achieved at each age. For documentation purposes, you must be able to meet this definition.

SOME TERMS USED IN TEST RESULTS

The following are some terms you may hear in the discussion of your test results. These definitions may help you to understand your diagnosis more completely.

Diagnostic tests: This series of formal and informal measures of skills and abilities, including general levels of intelligence and academic skill, is designed to identify your strengths and weaknesses and to assist in finding ways to help you learn and work more effectively.

Norm: This term is used a lot by test administrators when they are reading your scores back. They may say, "Well, your score falls between these norms." Establishing norms is an important step in standardizing a test. Many of the tests used to diagnose learning disabilities have no predetermined standards of passing or failing. In most cases, a person's test score is interpreted by comparing it with the scores of other people of the same age on the same test. Therefore, the norm is the normal or average performance. For example, if the average 17-year-old gets 77 out of 100 problems correct on a test, then the norm score for a 17-year-old is 77.

Normal: Although I hate this word, you will often hear it when talking to college administrators. They may say, "Well, we really need to see how you will perform compared to normal college freshmen with your major." Or from professors: "If I give you extra time on the exam, that will interfere with the academic integrity of the course that the normal students are challenged with." When this word is used, it implies that those who are learning disabled are **not** normal. If you hear this term, correct the speaker and assert that you are just as normal as other students. You just learn differently and need a different method of teaching and test taking.

Criterion-referenced: This term simply means that the validity of the instrument (the test) is measured against a criterion or standard. Therefore, test performance may be measured in terms of the specific kinds of mathematical skills mastered, the difficulty level of the reading material comprehended, or the estimated vocabulary size. In this way, a specified content area is used as an interpretive frame of reference for the instrument, instead of a specified population of test takers.

Standardization: This term implies the uniformity of procedure in administering and scoring the test. Telling people that you "don't do well on standardized tests" is a very logical thing to say, because a standardized test is given just that way—the standard way. Therefore, because you don't learn in the traditional or standard way, you probably don't perform well on a standardized test. You will, however, do better with a **dynamic assessment** or some sort of accommodation, like taking a test orally or using a scribe.

Dynamic assessment: This term may be used to explain your scores. Basically, it means that there was an intentional departure from the traditional or standardized way in which your test was administered.

My Experience: I hate taking tests; I don't test well. But there were times when I had to be tested, just as you have been or will be. The last time I was tested, my examiner used this dynamic assessment method, so I had a better opportunity to show what I could do. Then I was tested without the dynamic assessment, so the administrator could compare the scores. Using testing methods that deviated slightly from the traditional ones made a big difference for me. For example, since I am a very tactile and visual learner, allowing me to use paper and pencil for the math section helped me do much better. Having this option to work out the math problems physically gave me the same level playing field as test takers who don't have a learning disability.

Attention Deficit/Hyperactivity Disorder (ADHD) or Hyperactivity: A person with ADHD moves constantly and is restless much of the time. This person talks a lot and many times has incomplete thoughts, because his or her thoughts often run together. Sometimes this person may have poor motor control and coordination. This person also gets frustrated quickly, can be moody, and is easily distracted.

Hypoactivity: The hypoactive individual works and reacts slowly. This person appears unemotional and will hang onto a task even when it is completed.

Attention Deficit Disorder (ADD): Someone with ADD has many of the same symptoms as someone with ADHD, but without the hyperactivity. For example, a person with ADD daydreams and is confused much of the time and never seem to finish tasks or projects. He or she gets bored very easily; concentration for this person is a monumental task. Distracted by other people and by outside noises, this person can be moody and unpredictable.

FOR FURTHER READING

Lyon, R. (1994). <u>Frames of reference for the assessment of learning disabilities: New views on measurement issues</u>. Baltimore: Paul H. Brookes Publishing.

Kavale, K., & Forness, S. (1995). <u>The nature of learning disabilities: Critical elements of diagnosis and classification</u>. Hillsdale, NJ: Lawrence Erbaum.

Chapter 4
TAKING THE SAT OR ACT

THE SAT

As a sophomore in high school, I remember seeing a friend of mine very intently reading a study guide for the Preliminary Scholastic Aptitude Test (PSAT). This test helps you practice for taking the SAT and is the National Merit Scholarship qualifying test. I was not registered to take the PSAT. My friend told me that I should have registered to take the PSAT, so I would have an idea of what to expect on the SAT. I wanted to say, "get a life," but I knew deep in my heart that she **would** have a life, probably of a much better quality than mine, because at that time I didn't even know if I was going to graduate from high school.

Administered since 1926 by the Educational Testing Service (ETS), the Scholastic Aptitude Test is the college entrance exam most often required for college admission. When I was in high school, I remember dreading the SAT. I was intimidated by tests anyway, as are most learning-disabled individuals, but this was an important timed exam—even scarier!

Any person with a documented learning disability can get accommodations for taking the PSAT and the SAT, including extra time. If I could do it again, I would take the PSAT. Had I gone into the SAT knowing what to expect, I might have done better on it. Also, had I known that I was entitled to take extra time, or request a reader on the test, I would have done so.

Tips and Useful Information

- ✎ You and your counselor should start the application process early for taking the PSAT and/or the SAT using accommodations. I recommend that you begin this process the spring before the year you are planning to take the test.

- ✎ You must get a "common eligibility form" from the College Board. The College Board Services for Students with Disabilities (SSD) provides testing accommodations for the SAT as well as the PSAT.

- ✎ You can use this form for all tests administered by the College Board. Your school also completes a part of this form.

- ✎ Once approved, you will be sent a letter of eligibility that states that you can have accommodations. Your school will get a copy of this letter as well.

- ✎ Examples of the types of accommodations you might be given are extended time, a proctor or reader, and specific color background and/or foreground for certain visual and reading disabilities.

- ✎ You can also have computer and technology accommodations if you are taking the computer-based test. These kinds of accommodations, however, have to be specified and documented.

- ✎ You can use alternate testing formats.

- ✎ In all cases, you must be able to meet all the requirements for documentation of your learning disability.

- ✎ Your documentation must be current (not older than three years), have been done by a qualified professional, and include a specific diagnosis.

- ✎ You should know that the testing professional must also make recommendations for accommodations and give the reasons for making them. Most importantly, the documentation must indicate that your learning disability substantially limits the major life function of learning.

- ✎ Pay close attention to registration deadlines for test applications. Often, those who are requesting accommodations must register early.

✎ Before you begin this process, be sure to consult the ETS web site, http://www.ets.org, to see if the Office of Disability has made any changes in its policies.

✎ Chapter 3 ("Documenting Your Learning Disability") may also help you.

THE ACT

The American College Test (ACT) is your other choice for an admissions test. First given in 1959, the ACT is administered by the American College Testing Program, based in Iowa City. The ACT is most often used by colleges in the Midwest and western United States, and less often used by colleges on the East Coast. Some colleges allow you to take either the SAT or the ACT.

 **My Experience:** If you have a choice, I recommend taking the ACT. It seemed to be more "user-friendly" than the SAT. I scored higher on it, as did most of the other students with learning disabilities I have talked to.

Tips and Useful Information

✎ You and your counselor should start the application process early for taking the ACT and/or the PACT with accommodations. I recommend that you begin this process the spring before the year you are planning on taking the test.

✎ You must provide documentation just as you would for accommodations in college. The ACT Office of Services for Students with Disabilities states on its website, "If you currently receive accommodations in school due to a professionally diagnosed and documented disability, you may provide documentation to support your request for accommodations."

Accommodations Available for the ACT

You should familiarize yourself with the following accommodations.

Standard Time-National Testing with Accommodations. ACT refers to this as Option #1. This means that you can take the test with the standard time limits, but you use either a standard or large print test booklet, and your disability requires accommodations at the testing location, for example, a room with no distractions by others taking the test. Using this option means your test scores will be marked "National." I explain this kind of marking later as "Flagging the Test."

Documentation for this option specifically requires that you have a professional explain the nature of your disability in detail and the accommodations that you normally receive in school.

Extended-Time National Testing. ACT refers to this as Option #2. This means that you can test at a regularly scheduled test center and use either a standard or large print test booklet, but you require additional time due to your professionally diagnosed and documented disability. Using this option means that your test scores will be marked "Special." The extended time allotted is up to five hours total testing time, including your breaks between test sections. This is more than time and a half—the standard for extended time on a standardized test. This option usually means that you will be assigned a separate room and a private proctor.

Documentation for this option consists of a special application you and your school official fill out. This application will require your diagnosis and the appropriate documentation.

Non-National Testing Option. This option is good if you normally—meaning in your current school situation—use more than 50% additional time for tests, or you require testing over more than one day because of your disability, or you use alternate test formats such as using a reader or an audio cassette. If you use this option, your test scores will be marked "Special."

You and your school official will have to complete a request for ACT Assessment Special Testing. This request should include documentation of your diagnosed disability and all supporting information. Your school officials and/or counselors can obtain all special forms and applications.

I recommend that you look at the ACT web site, http://www.act.org, for updated information on policies regarding testing accommodations and registration.

FLAGGING AND DISCLOSURE

It is important to realize that when you take either the SAT or the ACT with accommodations for your learning disability, your test scores will be "flagged," or specially marked. This means that your results will include a statement about the testing conditions. For example, as I stated in the section regarding the ACT, if you take the test using Option #1, your scores will be marked "National." To the college or university, this means that you took this test using the standard time given in national testing with accommodations.

The marking of your scores as "Special" tells the college or university that you took the test using the extended time option or the special testing with extended time and alternate test formats.

In the SAT, scores are marked or flagged as "Nonstandard Administration." If the test is administered with accommodations that do not require nonstandard time conditions, such as large print test or just a private room, then the scores are marked as "Nonstandard."

Other than these markings on reported scores, your disability and any other information that you provide is strictly confidential. The college or university should not and cannot ask you about your disability at the interview. You may want to disclose this information during the interview anyway to show how you have compensated for your disability and survived 12 years of education.

You may also want to disclose the disability on your application in the essay section. This way you have another opportunity to focus on your abilities despite your disabilities. If the college you want to enter requires that you apply to a separate LD program to get the services you need, then you will also be disclosing to them, of course. Separate programs for LD students are discussed in Chapter 5.

I know it seems unfair that your scores are marked differently because you are learning disabled, but keep in mind that because you will take your test under different conditions, your scores will be different. When these standardized tests are "normed" or studied in statistical reports on average SAT scores at a certain college or university, your scores cannot be considered in those statistics, because you took them in a nonstandard way. You are NOT part of the so-called norm here.

For Additional Information

I cannot overemphasize the importance of knowing your legal entitlements. The ADA is behind you, and you should let the two administering organizations know that even though they cannot "norm" the scores of learning disabled students, you are still entitled to take these tests with accommodations.

If you or your school counselor and school officials have any questions about the procedures for registering for these tests or obtaining accommodations, contact the two administering organizations:

American College Testing Program (ACT)
P. O. Box 168
Iowa City, IA 5224
319/337-1000
www.act.org

Educational Testing Service (SAT)
P. O. Box 6000
Princeton, NJ 08541-6000
609/921-9000
www.ets.org

Chapter 5

FINDING THE RIGHT COLLEGE FOR YOU

To find out whether something is right for you, you have to ask the right questions. When you buy a stereo, you probably ask lots of questions to find one that suits your needs, and the same is true when you are buying a car or any other big-ticket item. Think of college as a big-ticket item. When you are looking for a college, you are in the market for an education, and you should go to a school suited to your needs. You may be able to get into an Ivy League school, but if that school does not have the services to help you do well there, then it is not the right place for you. You must get accurate and complete information before you commit to any college or university.

Your choice of a college should be one that you feel strongly about. College is not just a place to get an education, but a home and lifestyle for four years or more. I went to many schools before I finally ended up at the university from which I graduated. That school not only had the services I needed, but a supportive environment in which I knew I could live and learn until I accomplished my goal.

As you make your choice, don't convince yourself that just because one college accepts you, that it is the only college that will. Take your time in making this decision. It is one that will affect you for at least the next four years—and possibly for the rest of your life. Here are some things you should consider before you make your final decision:

Does this college have a learning disabilities program, or does it provide services for the learning disabled under general disabled services?

This question is often a confusing one, because colleges can define learning disabilities programs in several different ways. Some colleges provide services for the learning disabled but no separate program for people with learning disabilities. Here is how I see the difference:

Learning disability program or structured program: A specific, full-time college or university program catering to the needs of the clinically recognized LD student. A college or university with a full-time program will usually have a full-time learning disability specialist, as well as the latest learning disability technology. A college with a specific LD program may have less technology and fewer services for people with learning disabilities than a school with a general student services office, however. Never assume that services will be provided.

Learning disability services: These services may appear at the college or university under one of the following headings: Disabled Student Services, Reading and Study Skills Laboratory, Educational Development, or Tutorial Services. The difference between these services and a separate LD program is that these services are not specifically for the learning disabled. The college's department or division of student services provides accommodations and assistance to all recognized disabilities. Therefore, they may not provide the latest equipment for LD students or have a learning disabilities specialist. But the school is still required to provide reasonable accommodations for any disabled student, including those with learning disabilities.

Which is better: a college with a program specifically geared toward learning disabled students, or a school that just has learning disability services?

Whether one school is better than another really depends on the college. Some colleges have great LD programs, but others have even better Disabled Student Services (DSS) departments. You must find out what makes a particular program special and whether it meets **your** needs.

You do need to be able to recognize what you need in terms of support at a college or university. Know your disability and how you learn best. If you are attending IEP meetings in your high school, this should be discussed. Listen to what your counselor, teacher, or LD specialist says and know what strategies are being put in place for you. This will help you decide what your needs are. Some if not all of these strategies can be duplicated at your college or university. For example, if you are using a note taker in your current classes, chances are you will need one in your college classes as well. But you must be aware of how you learn and under what circumstances you learn best.

My Experience: The college where I finally received my bachelor's and my master's degrees did not have a separate learning disabilities program. It did have very good services for disabled students, however, and by my senior year, it served more students with learning disabilities than students with any other disabilities. It also made a reading and writing center available for all students and had up-to-date adaptive equipment and computers. Most importantly, it had a learning disabilities specialist on staff. The Department of Disabled Student Services was the reason why I made it through college.

If the college or university has a separate LD program, do I need to apply to that program as well as to the college?

Often, such a program requires an admission procedure separate from that of the university or college. In most cases, you have to be admitted to the school before you are accepted into the LD program. Other students have been accepted into the LD program but rejected from the university itself. The answer to this question is important because you need to know if you will have to fill out two separate applications, and if so, whether you have different requirements and/or deadlines for each. You must call and speak to a staff person in the LD program.

What does the college or university require in terms of documentation to receive services?

You can get the answer to this question by calling the DSS office or LD program and speaking to the LD specialist or the person in charge of checking LD documentation. What assessments or tests does the school require as proof of a learning disability? Generally, the tests may not be over three years old.

Does the college have an added fee for use of the services for the learning disabled?

Believe it or not, some colleges require an additional payment for these services. Often this charge is to pay for tutors, a fee that non-learning disabled students also have to pay. On the other hand, these services are **your** accommodations. Do the colleges require the wheelchair-bound students to pay an additional fee for the use of wheelchair ramps? Since the passage of the ADA, students may begin to contest such fees in court to force colleges to lower these fees or waive them altogether. Having a disability should not mean you acquire an extra tax or fee.

If the college justifies this extra fee as payment for tutors and study skills classes for LD students, then I advise you to use the tutorial services to the limit, and request a tutor who has experience working with LD students. And go to those study skills classes!

Does the college or university provide any of the following accommodations: test proctors; extended time on exams; options to take oral, rather than written exams; note takers; use of tape recorders in class; textbooks on tape or readers for texts; use of computer screen reading systems; or advanced speech synthesizers?

These services and accommodations can make or break your success in college. Ask if the school provides these and any other services that will help you. If you need a multisensory approach to learning, find out what kind the college offers. For example, does the college provide hands-on learning opportunities in the curriculum—opportunities that allow for tactile as well as didactic learning? Can you utilize a note taker and/or audio tape classes? Speak to the LD specialist if there is one on staff, or speak to the director of the program.

What equipment, if any, does the college or university have for LD students? Ask for specifics. Does the college or university have a Kurzweil Reader on campus? A talking computer? A voice recognition system? A real-time spell checker?

Equipment and computer software can make a difference in the way you learn and the speed with which you do so. See Chapter 6 for a more complete list of equipment that may be helpful to you.

Does this college offer curriculum modification?

In other words, can you take another class instead of a foreign language? Or can a person with dyscalcula substitute a statistics requirement with a less complicated math course? LD students often drop out of school because they can't pass foreign language or math courses. Ask about what curriculum modifications will be available to you as a student with a learning disability. The answer to this question can make a big difference for you.

 **My Experience:** I was given the option of taking a class in foreign culture instead of a foreign language. Since I had already failed several foreign language classes, I cannot tell you how happy that made me. This opportunity was one of the things that helped save my college career.

Does the college have an option for completing a four-year degree program in five years or longer?

Many LD students (as well as others) find it difficult to manage a full course-load (usually between four and six classes a semester). This can make it hard to complete a degree in four years. As a result, some colleges now offer a five-year program. Knowing that you have the option of additional time can relieve some of the stress of your college experience.

 **My Experience:** It took me seven years to finish my bachelor's degree. Please remember, however, that this was my experience; this is not the average time for a student with a learning disability.

Keep in mind there can be financial ramifications to pursuing your degree over five years or more. Scholarships, grants, and loans may only be available over a certain time period. It is vitally important that you discuss this with your financial aid office before you decide to lengthen your college career.

Does the college have an LD support group or LD resource group?

You may benefit from getting together with other LD students once a week or twice a month. In such a group, you can discuss such things as getting through a particular class or dealing with a particular professor.

Such a group can help you find out which professors understand different learning styles and which ones are less accommodating as you select your courses. It also helps just to learn that you are not the only student having these difficulties and that others know what it's like to struggle through a class and still get just a "C."

This group can also act as a social vehicle for you: you will have a chance to make friends and to feel comfortable being around other people with the same or similar difficulties.

My Experience: I found the group at my college to be extremely helpful and supportive. Sometimes the group invited guest speakers to talk about issues that concerned us; other times the group held sessions to just vent and listen. I always found it much easier to talk about the problems I was having in the classroom or with my classwork to other people with learning disabilities. They always seemed to know what I was talking about. The group also created an "underground" list of professors to stay away from.

I have created a checklist with these questions that you can photocopy to use when calling or visiting colleges and universities. You can find this checklist in Appendix A.

OTHER OPTIONS: COMMUNITY OR JUNIOR COLLEGES

One option that you should not rule out is the community college, called a junior college in some areas. This type of school generally offers two-year programs with degrees that range from an associate's (AA) degree to a technical certificate.

The programs are generally quite varied, and a community college can offer a very supportive environment to the LD student. Furthermore, a community college can build a foundation from which to transfer to a four-year college and obtain a bachelor's degree. The classes in community colleges are usually smaller and give students more opportunities to meet one-on-one with professors.

 **My Experience:** The community college I attended did not have a learning disability specialist or a learning disability center, but it did have one counselor who was responsible for all the disabled students. At this college, I arranged for all my exams ahead of time and took them in the counseling center with a proctor, who was usually the counselor. I enjoyed the smaller classes, and I got more individual attention from the instructors.

Often, a student will choose to go to a community college before attending a four-year program—whether or not he or she has a learning disability—because the costs are lower. You should keep college expenses in mind because, as a learning disabled student, you may take longer than four years to finish a bachelor's degree. If so, you will have more than four years of tuition bills or student loans to pay back. To keep those costs down, you might consider a two-year program, if just for financial reasons. The quality of the education at an accredited two-year college can be just as high and can help prepare you for a four-year college or university. Moreover, most four-year institutions will accept up to 60 credits for transfer from a two-year college. Four-year colleges usually require around 120 credits to graduate, so transferring 60 credits into a school will put you well on your way to a degree. You might want to check with your intended four-year college, however. The specifics of which credits will transfer do vary from school to school. You don't want to have to repeat classes, which can be time-consuming and expensive.

In many cases, if you attend a community or junior college and you earn 30 credits or more and then transfer to a four-year college, you will not need SAT scores. A four-year college or university will admit you on the basis of your grades in the courses you transfer.

While many two-year colleges may not have a learning disabilities specialist, a learning disability center, or services specifically geared toward LD students on campus, you do have the right to accommodations for your learning disability at community colleges, just as you do at a four-year college or university. Any community college probably has an office for disabled students, so be sure to tell your advisor or counselor about your diagnosis and provide appropriate documentation.

The community college is also an option if you want to take a class in the summer. When you return home from your college or university, or even before you return, look into the summer schedule at the local community college. The summer is a perfect time for taking a class you need at time when you don't have to worry about all your other classes.

Furthermore, a community college near your college or university may offer a class you are required to take during a time when your college doesn't offer it. To make sure that the class is equivalent to the one at your institution, you will need to get approval from your college advisor and/or department head to take the class. This is usually just a matter of bringing in the class description from the community college catalogue. It's a good idea to get this approval before you register for the class, though, to make sure it's equivalent to the required class at your college or university.

Most importantly, the community college can be a place to get remedial work, which is a good thing to know.

FEEL PASSIONATE ABOUT YOUR SCHOOL CHOICE

This is very important! I strongly advocate that you visit the schools you are applying to before you make a final choice. Decide what learning climate will be best for you, not just what your parents or your friends recommend to you. **You** are the one who will have to be there for four or more years and **you** will be the one expected to succeed.

RESOURCES TO HELP YOU

Many colleges can cater to your specific learning needs. In addition to the list of LD-friendly colleges in Appendix B, the following guides list and evaluate colleges with services for the learning disabled.

Kraviets, M., & I.F. Wax. (1998).The K & W Guide to Colleges for the Learning Disabled (4th ed.). New York: Harper Perennial.

This guide is the best you can buy. It is very complete and easy to follow. Many authors and editors of similar guides do not realize that the LD student is often the reader, so the guide must be easy to read and to follow. The authors of this guide have written it with the learning disabled reader in mind.

The K & W Guide gives a full description of the colleges in an easy-to-follow format. For every school listed, it covers 66 points on everything from the type of support the college provides (learning disability structured program or coordinated services), to the kind of athletic program it has. It also gives such vital information as the kind of LD equipment (such as Kurzweil Readers) available to students and the availability of textbooks on tape or readers to tape textbooks. The guide also gives tuition and housing information. In addition, it lists two-year colleges. Overall, it is very thorough and complete.

Mangrum, C. T. & S.S. Strichart. (1997). Peterson's Colleges with Programs for Students with Learning Disabilities. Princeton, NJ: Peterson's Guides, Inc.

This guide is much harder to follow and is really geared for the school counselor, not the student. The guide's best point, however, is that it is divided into two sections: one listing colleges with comprehensive programs and the other listing colleges with special services. It is fairly thorough and gives such information as whether colleges offer alternative exam arrangements and whether it has a learning disabled support group. It is also helpful to those serving the LD population. A bonus CD is included.

PART TWO

SURVIVING COLLEGE

Classroom 102

Chapter 6

ASSISTIVE TECHNOLOGY FOR THE LEARNING DISABLED

More new technologies to assist the learning disabled are being designed every day. Just since I finished graduate school in 1995, a flood of new products has entered the marketplace. Some of these technologies were originally developed for the deaf, the hearing impaired, or the visually impaired, but these technologies can often benefit the learning disabled population as well.

Keeping up on the latest equipment and knowing what technology will suit your learning needs can be a full-time job. One helpful resource for this information is <u>Assistive Technology for People with Disabilities</u>, by Dianne Pedrotty Bryant and Brian R. Bryant (Allyn & Bacon, 2002). Its collection of articles focusing on the use of computer technology for the learning disabled can be a valuable resource in purchasing adaptive technology for college. The articles are not only useful in an educational setting, but in the workplace as well. The book is written for a diverse audience, including educators, researchers, and manufacturers, as well as parents and adults with learning and/or physical disabilities.

MULTISENSORY APPROACHES TO READING

Books on Tape

One option that helped save me in college was books on tape from **Recordings for the Blind and Dyslexic (RFB&D)**. Originally called Recordings for the Blind, the organization changed its name as more people with learning disabilities began to use this service. When I first heard about this service, I thought, "I'm not blind. What could this organization do for me?" It didn't take long to figure it out. Some learning disabled people don't perceive written words in a way they can easily read. The words on the page appear jumbled or backward and fall off the page. We can't keep our place and often end up reading the same line for an hour. The beauty of books on tape is that you can listen instead. I find it helpful to listen and follow along with my finger or with a blocker of some sort.

The way RFB&D works is pretty simple. You'll need to send an application that will register you as an RFB&D user (see the end of this chapter for contact information). You must pay a one-time fee to register and an annual membership fee. In addition, the organization requires a disability statement certifying that you do indeed qualify for its services. This statement can come from your Disabled Student Services coordinator, the learning disability specialist who works with you at your college, your vocational rehabilitation counselor, or your high school special education teacher or counselor. After you are registered with RFB&D, you can submit requests for books on tape for the rest of your school career. The tapes are shipped at no cost to you, and other than the cost of membership, the service is free. You are **borrowing** these tapes; return labels will be enclosed so you can ship them back to RFB&D when you are done with them. There is no set time limit; RFB&D expects that you will be borrowing a textbook throughout a semester. You will receive reminders, however, that you have a borrowed book.

Occasionally, RFB&D will not have a textbook that you need, or they will have a different edition than the one you require for your course. If so, the organization will write you to let you know. In this case, check with the Office of Disabled Student Services (DSS) at your school to see if they can provide readers for you. Sometimes DSS has work-study students who proctor test sessions and record textbooks for the visually impaired and for learning-disabled students.

It is extremely important to request books from RFB&D well in advance, because it takes a long time to get the tapes shipped to you. This delay is especially long if the textbook is not already taped or if they need your approval to record a different edition of the book.

In 1991, RFB&D merged with Computerized Books for the Blind and expanded their library by more than 200 titles available on computer disks. The computerized texts cost $15 to $20 per title on average, but they are yours to keep, so you do not have to mail them back.

Tape Players and Other Accessories

Tapes (as opposed to computer disks) from RFB&D require a special kind of tape player that plays 15/16 inches per second (IPS) to accommodate two or four tracks. Your public library or school library probably has one that you can borrow.

Those who are eligible for services of the **National Library Service for the Blind and Physically Handicapped (NLS)**, a division of the U.S. Library of Congress, can request the playback equipment on loan for as long as patrons use the NLS library service. Go to your local library or school library and ask if you can apply for NLS borrowing services. The NLS will allow only RFB&D borrowers and patrons of NLS to borrow equipment. You should consult your regional NLS network library for more information. NLS also produces a buying guide that lists all the known sources for adaptive equipment.

The **American Printing House for the Blind (APH)** also sells tape players and accessories. These tape players are a good option, because they also record and can be used to tape class lectures as well. The players sold through APH are easy to carry around. The equipment from NLS tends to be much older, bulkier versions of the 4-track cassette players that are impossible to carry around in your bookbag. For information on the price, size, and availability of equipment, contact APH at the address and phone number at the end of this chapter.

RFB&D also sells the tape players you need for these tapes. They have four portable models and four desktop models from which to choose.

Contact information for all of these organizations appears at the end of this chapter.

The Kurzweil Reader

The **Kurzweil Reader** is a computer that scans printed material and then reads aloud, in one of six voices chosen by the user, what it has scanned. Although it was developed mainly for use by the visually impaired, the device is extremely useful to LD students.

My Experience: My university purchased the Kurzweil Reader for the visually impaired. The LD students also made good use of it, however. Many times, I realized that I didn't have a reader for some articles that I needed to read by my next class, sometimes by that afternoon. I would go to the library where the equipment was kept, put my article on the scanner, pick the voice, the speed, and the format—and bingo! The article was read to me. I frequently brought a tape recorder so that I could tape the reading as well. It was fast and easy.

The Kurzweil Reader is an invaluable piece of technology. Be sure to find out if your college has this or something similar available for students.

COMPUTERS AND SOFTWARE

Access to Computers at School

Most schools have computer labs available to all students. If you have not already discovered it for yourself, you will find that basic computer knowledge will make a huge difference in your life and in your learning. If you can afford your own computer, by all means, buy one. You will be glad to have your own machine and not have to worry about computer availability in a crowded lab. It is great to be able to have your customized software on it as well.

Some DSS offices have computers with adaptive software on them. Check out the available adaptive equipment for LD students at all the colleges you are considering. Believe me, having the right equipment can make learning easier for you throughout your college years. Though technology will not cure your learning disability, it will increase your access to an equal education.

Useful Software

The market is literally exploding with LD-friendly software. There is so much out there that by the time you read this, there will be many more programs than the ones I mention. Also keep in mind that the ones to which I refer here are the ones that I like. This does not mean that they will work for you. I know what my needs are in an educational setting (and now a work setting), so I look at software with which I am familiar and that fits my learning needs.

You are the consumer here, so be absolutely certain that the product you buy will work for you. Ask lots of questions, and get all the information you can on the product before you make a purchase. It is imperative that you ensure that your computer has the minimum system requirements to run the program you buy. Even more importantly, test the program before you buy it. Software retailers frequently offer demonstrations of programs to consumers; be sure you take advantage of these.

I'll focus on a few software programs that assist you in writing and reading to give you an idea of what is out there and what types of things to look for.

My Experience: As a graduate student, I was introduced to a voice-recognition computer program. Students were allowed to check out laptop computers with the software on them and take the computers to classes to take notes and exams. We were also allowed to use them for writing papers.

The program I used allowed me to hear what I was typing. As I typed, the speech synthesizer would speak and the highlighter would highlight each word. This allowed me to hear what I was typing. With a set of headphones, I was golden during essay exams or taking notes in class. My writing certainly improved when I used the system—and I even enjoyed writing more. I had become so tired of WordPerfect telling me that it could not recognize a word in spellcheck. With this system, I could often hear my misspellings. Another advantage was the highlighting, which really helped me to stay focused and not lose my place as often.

This particular voice-recognition program is now out of production, but there are many others on the market that function similarly. These programs can really help!

✎ One of the most popular programs in this category is **Dragon Systems Naturally Speaking Preferred™**. This is a continuous speech voice recognition software that types what you dictate and can read your documents back to you. It supports virtually all Windows applications. You can train the program with your voice in five minutes. When you speak into it, your voice is transcribed almost immediately and appears as text on the screen. You can use this program to write reports and papers, which is extremely important and helpful, but you can also use it for your e-mail or for browsing online.

✎ **Kurzweil 3000™** reads scanned or electronic text aloud using human-sounding synthetic speech. As they are spoken, the words are highlighted on the screen. The program recognizes voice commands also. Some colleges have this program available for student use, so be sure to ask.

✎ Another voice-recognition program is **L&H Voice Xpress™**. It allows you to dictate, format, and edit reports, letters, e-mails, and pretty much anything else you will need for school into all Windows applications. You can teach it your voice in virtually minutes, and the program will recognize up to 160 words per minute.

✎ **Via Voice™** is a voice-to-text/text-to-speech system that has been on the market for some time. Affordable and easy to install, it requires a short training time and has very fast text entry. This system allows you to dictate directly into word processing programs like Microsoft Word. It reads your typed and dictated text back to you, and you can edit and format your documents using your voice. All Via Voice editions have a neat feature called "Analyze My Documents," which learns and remembers how you write. The system has automatic formatting for dates, currency, weights, and phone numbers.

Via Voice comes in several editions:

– **Via Voice Standard™.**

– **Via Voice Personal™** allows you to create a Personal Voice Model that you can customize for greater dictation accuracy.

– **Via Voice Pro™** supports common office applications like Microsoft Outlook and Lotus SmartSuite in addition to word processing programs. It also has templates for faxes, memos, and business letters.

– **Via Voice Advanced™** has advanced speech recognition technology, so you can capture ideas and words by saying them at a normal speaking rate. You don't have to pause between words to allow the computer to keep up. It also supports additional programs, including Internet applications, and comes with specialized vocabulary topics built into its dictionary.

Each edition has different features and different system requirements, as well as a different retail price, so make sure you purchase the one that will best fulfill your needs.

Designed for and field-tested by LD students and adults, Freedom Scientific's **WYNN™ (What You Need Now) Wizard, Reader, and Interface** are excellent products. With WYNN Wizard you can scan any document and have it read to you or modify it by dictating or typing. WYNN Reader has all the same features except scanning capability. Both programs use WYNN's specially designed interface, which uses four different icon-driven, color-coded toolbars to allow you to customize your computer to suit your needs. The interface will spotlight each word as it reads the word aloud, and you can shut the voice off if you prefer visual input only. You can also change the size and spacing of text. If you find it difficult to follow word-to-word, the WYNN program can mask out distracting sections of the page or change the color of the cursor. You can easily highlight and insert bookmarks, and you can add written or spoken notes so that you can summarize important passages or sections. The dual auditory/visual presentation is probably one of the best features, and the color-coded toolbars are also very user-friendly. All the speech can be modified to fit your needs. It comes with Via Voice. Freedom Scientific (formerly Arkenstone) will let you try this for 30 days with a money-back guarantee. They also provide a one-year warranty.

✎ **textHELP! V6 GOLD™** is designed specifically for persons with reading and writing difficulties. It features screen reading, speech input, advanced phonetic spellchecker, contextual word prediction, abbreviation expansion, a log that will record typical spelling errors for future analysis, and a separate database that stores homophones, or like-sounding words. textHELP! comes with a toolbar that "floats" on top of any open application. You can also purchase a product called **Wordsmith** to add the textHELP! toolbar to your copy of Microsoft Word 97/2000.

✎ **Scan and Read™**, by Premier Programming Solutions, is a relatively low-cost scan-to-voice package. The program has templates that allow you to scan only the parts of a document that you need, rather than the whole thing. It can read existing files, as well as scanned documents. This program requires a screen reader like WindowEyes or Jaws for Windows; these are sold separately.

✎ **The Complete Reading System™**, also by Premier Programming Solutions, is a self-contained scan-to-voice program. It has many of the same functions as Scan and Read, but it does not require a screen reader. Most of the major functions can be operated with one keystroke, and this program supports a wide range of word processing programs.

OTHER TECHNOLOGY

Sometimes, when you are in a hurry, you may not be able to use a computer. You may want to jot down a note, a message, or get the correct spelling of a word.

My Experience: If you're like me, you may write the note on the nearest piece of paper and then later be unable to read your handwriting. Taking a telephone message for my roommates was particularly frustrating. Often, the caller would not slow down and would have already hung up before I could ask him or her to repeat the message. I'd get the dates and times backwards and my roommates would have a hard time reading my handwriting. I became very unpopular as a message taker. A gadget like the Language Master would have allowed me to punch in the message and store it correctly so that I could read it back to my roommate.

✎ **The Franklin Language Master™**, a portable note taker, dictionary, thesaurus, and spellchecker with speech capability, solves the problem. This little device reads and spells words and messages out loud, or pronounces them syllable by syllable. You can store up to 26 messages at a time, and the contrast and font size are adjustable, as is the speech speed. The Franklin Language Master comes with headphones, batteries, and an AC adapter.

A lot of other small accessories can help you get through your classes. For example, talking calculators can make that freshman algebra and those formulas in chemistry and physics go a bit easier.

My Experience: On a chemistry or physics test, I often would copy the wrong answer from my calculator. I copied what I saw, and it was usually backwards or scrambled. Sometimes I could convince a professor that I had done the problem right, but just copied the answer incorrectly from my calculator. Often, though, hard-nosed professors were worried about academic integrity and could not be convinced. A gadget like a talking calculator would have made all that unnecessary.

✎ Another rather cool piece of technology is the **Quicktionary Reading Pen II™** by Seiko Instruments. I got to try this out at an educational conference. It was the best thing I had used to read with in a long time. I thought about how many times I could have used this in a class when trying to read a handout that was given out during a lecture. Use this portable device to scan a word or line of text, and it displays the words in large characters on a digital screen on the side of the pen. It will read the word out loud, (you can plug in earphones), and it will even define the word aloud if you need it to. The display will even flip over for left-handed people!

✎ **The QuickLink Pen™** is an electronic highlighter that lets you copy, clip, and store printed text, Internet links, tables, and charts from any printed source and transfer the data to your computer, PDA (PalmPilot), or text-enabled cell phone. You can scan information directly into any Windows-based application or store up to 1000 pages and transfer it at your convenience.

Helpful Hints

Do your research thoroughly when looking for software and other technology to use in school. Be a smart shopper. Make sure you buy a product that suits your learning needs, and if you're buying software, be certain that your computer will support the program you are buying.. Comparison shop as much as possible to ensure you're getting the best deal—and don't forget to look online!

If you purchase adaptive technology, you may be eligible for some form of reimbursement. Your school may cover some or all of it, or you may be eligible for an outside program. Locating the funds is time consuming, however. You must be able to assess your own resources and determine whether you meet the eligibility requirements for publicly funded programs. **The National Rehabilitation Information Center (NARIC)** can be a great source of information about both purchasing adaptive equipment and getting reimbursed for it. NARIC's Funding Sources Checklist may help you find ways to fund such purchases.

If you are not too sure about some of these technologies or if you want to stay aware of new and upcoming technology, I recommend that you join an organization called the **Rehabilitation Engineering and Assistive Technology Society of North America (RESNA)**, an interdisciplinary association for the advancement of rehabilitation and assistive technologies. RESNA provides two very informative publications: the quarterly journal Assistive Technology, and RESNA News. You will probably be interested in the material under "special education," which covers information on assistive technology for the education of young people.

Descriptions and contact information for many other helpful organizations appear at the end of this chapter.

LESS EXPENSIVE STUDY AIDS

As this chapter on technology for the LD began to unfold, I realized how expensive LD technology is. Let's face it—the software and equipment I have talked about is pricey, and this is bad news if you are a struggling college student. Believe me, I know what it means to live on a student budget. Pay attention to this next section for some technology tips that won't bankrupt you.

Tinted Overlays

This item, found at any art store, is a piece of tinted plastic or overlay. Also referred to as a blocker, this device is simply placed over whatever piece of text you are reading. It helps me get much more out of what I am trying to learn because I can follow along with my text as I am listening to my tapes.

I first read about this technique in September 1990 in an article called "Simple Treatment May Aid Dyslexics" in USA Today. When I told a counselor about it (Betty W., wherever you are, thanks!), she looked for this colored plastic, found it, and gave me a manila envelope full of red plastic overlays. The red ones work best for me, but other LD students I know like to use blue or green.

Once I started using this overlay, I noticed that my reading speed went up. Even at times when I didn't have the tape of a book or an article to follow, my speed improved. When I did have a tape, my reading and listening speeds both increased with the use of this very inexpensive tool.

Over the years I have read more about this technique, known as the Irlen method. These overlays, referred to as Irlen filters, are named for Helen Irlen, an American educational psychologist who presented a paper on them at the 1983 Annual Convention of the American Psychological Association. Studies show that these filters do work well for some people with reading disabilities.

According to the Irlen Institute, the overlays work for some people with learning disabilities because "the tinted filters filter specific light frequencies and remove a range of perceptual disorders that adversely affect reading and related learning performance." These disorders are now known as Scotopic Sensitivity/Irlen Syndrome. The Irlen Institute states that you should be tested to see if these overlays will work. If you do have Irlen Syndrome, a perceptual dysfunction, then other treatments may help you as well. But I encourage you to try the filters on your own and see if it makes a difference.

Specialized Optometrists

Something else that can make a difference (and won't be as expensive as some of the other technologies I've discussed) is consulting a developmental optometrist. When I was in college, my vocational rehabilitation counselor (I will talk about the role of the vocational rehabilitation counselor in your life later) suggested that I see a developmental optometrist, an eye doctor whose specialty is working with people who have developmental reading disabilities.

My Experience: I needed prisms in my reading glasses to help with my reading. The way I understand it, the prisms help to defract the print from the paper and spread it over the retina in such a way that I can process it as one image.

Also, because I was a client of vocational rehabilitation, that agency paid for my first appointment and $100 on the glasses.

I highly recommend at least one visit to a developmental optometrist just to see if some kind of glasses can help you.

RESOURCES

Books on Tape and Accessories

✎ **American Printing House for the Blind (APH)**
P. O. Box 6085
Louisville, KY 40206-0085
502/895-2405
www.aph.org

✎ **National Library Service for the Blind and Physically Handicapped (NLS)**
The Library of Congress
Washington, DC 20542
202/287-5927
www.loc.gov/nls
(also inquire at your local library for borrowing information)

✎ **Recordings for the Blind and Dyslexic (RFB&D)**
The Anne T. Macdonald Center
20 Roszel Road
Princeton, NJ 08540
866/RFBD-585
www.rfbd.org

Computer Software Manufacturers and Distributors

✎ **Creative Labs**
800/998-5227
Fax: 405/624-6780
www.americas.creative.com

✎ **Freedom Scientific (formerly Arkenstone)**
888/223-3344 or 650/475-5435
www.freedomscientific.com
wynn@freedomscientific.com

✎ **Inclusive Technology for Special Needs People**
www.inclusive.co.uk

✎ **Kurzweil Educational Systems, Inc.**
14 Crosby Drive
Bedford, MA 01730-1402
800/894-5374
www.kurzweiledu.com

✎ **Next Generation Technologies**
www.ngtvoice.com

✎ **Pulse Data HumanWare**
175 Mason Circle
Concord, CA 94520
800/722-3393
Fax: 925/681-4630
www.humanware.com

✎ **Quicktionary Reading Pen**
888/777-0552
www.wizcomtech.com

✎ **ScanSoft (owns both L&H and Dragon Systems)**
800/654-1187
Fax: 978/977-2434
www.scansoft.com/products

✎ **Speech Technology, Inc**
www.speechtechnology.com

✎ **textHELP!**
888/333-9907
www.texthelp.com

Other Organizations

✎ **ABLEDATA:** This rich electronic database of information on assistive technology and rehabilitation equipment available in the United States, funded by the National Institute on Disability and Rehabilitation Research of the U.S. Department of Education. With more than 23,000 product listings, ABLEDATA covers everything from white canes and adaptive clothing to low-vision reading systems and voice output programs. Each product record provides a detailed description of the item, complete company contact information, and distributor listings (where applicable). In addition to commercially available products, the database also lists noncommercial prototypes, customized products, and one-of-a-kind products. This site also provides a collection of assistive technology fact sheets and consumer guides.
www.abledata.com

✎ **The ADAPTECH Project:** The Project consists of a team of academics, students, and consumers conducting research on the use of computer, information, and adaptive technologies by Canadian college and university students with disabilities. It is based at Dawson College. Their goal is to provide research-based information to other colleges and universities to ensure that their new policies, software and hardware reflect the needs and concerns of a variety of individuals: college and university students with disabilities, professors who teach them, and service providers who make technological, adaptive, and other supports available to the higher education community.
http://adaptech.dawsoncollege.qc.ca/

✎ **Assistive Technology for Postsecondary Students with Learning Disabilities:** This article by Sheryl L. Day and Barbara J. Edwards was published in the Journal of Learning Disabilities, (September, 1996). This is an informational piece on how technology can be used to help meet the educational demands of students with learning disabilities at the postsecondary level, including need for technology training in transition planning.
www.ldonline.org/ld_indepth/technology/postsecondary_tech.html

✎ **Apple—Special Needs:** Apple provides a series of disability-related information resources. This site explains the Universal Access features that are built into the Macintosh operating system.
www.apple.com/disability

✎ **Center for IT Accommodation (CITA):** A nationally recognized model demonstration facility influencing accessible information environments, services, and management practices.
www.itpolicy.gsa.gov/cita/index.htm

✎ **Center for Applied Special Technology (CAST):** CAST is a not-for-profit organization whose mission is to expand opportunities for individuals with disabilities through innovative uses of computer technology. It pursues this mission through research and product development that further universal design for learning. CAST serves a national population of children and adults who have learning disabilities, physical challenges, sensory deficits, and who represent a wide variation in socio-economic status, including those who have been traditionally underserved.
www.cast.org

✎ **The Closing the Gap Library (CTG):** CTG is an internationally recognized source for information on innovative applications of computer technology in special education and rehabilitation. I've used this guide to get price information and descriptions of equipment both as a student and for my clients as a professional. Its extensive online resource library contains articles in the following 23 categories: Assessment, Augmentative Communication, Curriculum Development, Early Childhood, Employment, Environmental Control, Funding, Geriatrics, IEP/IPP, Inclusion, Internet, Keyboard Alternatives, Language Development, Learning Styles, Literacy, Multimedia, Screen Alternatives, Seating Positioning & Mobility, Software Adaptation, Teacher/Parent Training, Technology Integration, Telecommunications, and Transition.
www.closingthegap.com

✎ **DO-IT:** The Disabilities, Opportunities, Internetworking, and Technology Program at the University of Washington is partially funded by the National Science Foundation. It offers many resources, including a compilation of mailing lists, Usenet discussion groups,

electronic newsletters, websites, and gopher servers containing information of interest to people with disabilities.
www.washington.edu/doit/

✎ **Dyslexic.com:** This is a great website for dyslexia and technology updates. **www.dyslexic.com**
e-mail: sales@dyslexic.com

✎ **Irlen Institute:** This organization provides comprehensive information about Irlen Syndrome and Irlen filters.
www.irlen.com
Info@Irlen.com

✎ **Job Accommodation Network (JAN):** This toll-free consulting service provides information about job accommodations and employability of people with disabilities. JAN also can provide information on the Americans with Disabilities Act (ADA).
800/526-7234
janweb.icdi.wvu.edu

✎ **Microsoft Accessibility:** This site describes Microsoft's accessibility efforts, accessibility features on all of its products, and accessibility aids produced by other companies, along with a listing of articles on accessibility and other related information.
www.microsoft.com/enable

✎ **The National Center to Improve Practice In Special Education Through Technology, Media and Materials (NCIP):** NCIP, funded by the U.S. Department of Education, Office of Special Education Programs, promotes the effective use of technology to enhance educational outcomes for students with sensory, cognitive, physical and social/emotional disabilities. The site is replete with helpful resources.
www2.edc.org/NCIP

✎ **RESNA:** Besides the two publications I mentioned earlier, RESNA also maintains a public domain software library and an electronic bulletin board. As a student member of this organization, you pay $50 for membership and the journal.
703/524-6686
TTY: 703/524-6639
www.resna.org

✎ **Selected Websites on Assistive Technology:** This site, compiled by the University of Delaware, contains links to other assistive technology resources.
www2.lib.udel.edu/atc/asstechn.htm

✎ **Tools for Life:** This organization is Georgia's assistive technology project and publishes <u>A Closer Look</u>, an assistive technology publication.
2 Peachtree St., Suite 35-415
Atlanta, GA 30303
800/497-8665
404/657-3084

✎ **The Trace Research & Development Center:** The Trace Center at the University of Wisconsin, Madison is one of the premier federally-funded research centers in the area of technology, disabilities, and accessibility.
www.tracecenter.org

Chapter 7

MANAGING YOUR TIME

Lots of college students have problems budgeting their time, but the learning disabled find it especially hard. We are not usually good estimators of a block of time—how long it will take to get something done or to go somewhere. It is very common for learning disabled students to be very early or very late for a class. We seem to have trouble grasping the distance from point A to point B and the time it will take to get there. To avoid over- or underestimating time, you will need to walk from your dorm or apartment to find out just how long it will take to get to your class or to take public transportation. Then you need to budget that traveling time into your everyday life.

Knowing how to manage your time is a skill. In fact, mastering this skill gives you the ability to **schedule** time, which in turn helps you **gain** time. Here are some things I have done that helped me manage my time well.

One thing that helped me organize my time was writing down all the things I did in one day and how much time it took to do them. It certainly made me realize that the amount of time I was spending studying for an upcoming exam was not nearly as much as I thought. I was also amazed at how long I took in the morning to drink a cup of coffee and get ready for the day. I also discovered that I had about two extra hours in the day that I didn't know about. I was using up too much time getting from my last class of the day to the subway because I spent a lot of it window-shopping and talking to my friends. I found a whole extra hour for studying if I walked straight to the subway and went home. By analyzing how you spend each day, you may find that the time you need is probably there. You just need to find it and put it to good use.

THE LD CALENDAR

Thinking of time in small blocks was something I also found helpful and much easier to grasp. Scheduling your day this way does not mean that you will never have free time. When you make up your schedule, you can plan your own free time. And when you begin to follow a structured timetable, you may find the free time you never thought you had. But don't forget the obvious things—like sleeping and eating.

Opposite is an example of a chart I use to help me keep my days and even my hours organized. You will find full-sized versions for photocopying in Appendix A.

This calendar has been a survival tool for me. I developed it slowly, as I learned from my mistakes and found what worked for me and what didn't. The syllabus that most professors give you on the first day of class will help you to turn your calendar into your own map for daily living and learning.

Let's review this calendar. First, notice the large amount of space for each hour. This calendar is not meant to be pocket-sized, something that you can just slip into your jeans and carry around with you. It is meant to be notebook-sized. Notice, too, that the calendar reads in blocks of time and begins at 7:00 A.M. You can fill in days and dates at the top of the page, so you won't be writing in the wrong activities or classes on the wrong day. I prefer to write the days of the week in red, but when you personalize the calendar, choose the color that's best for you. I highlight the times on mine in green, the color I found the clearest and most comfortable to read, next to the red dates and days. If you use a tinted overlay on the calendar, remember to use a different color pen or what you write will not show through. I recommend you copy the calendar, three-hole punch it, and then put it in a notebook, with the "Morning" page on the left-hand side.

When you open up the calendar pages to a day, you will see 7:00 A.M.– 8:00 P.M. facing you. This setup allows you to see the whole day at one glance

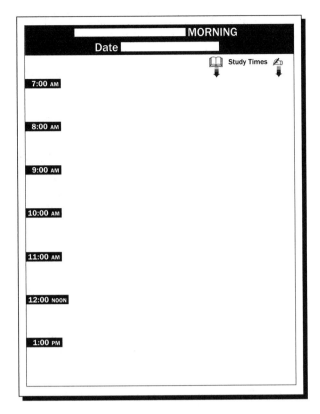

MORNING

Date

Study Times

7:00 AM

8:00 AM

9:00 AM

10:00 AM

11:00 AM

12:00 NOON

1:00 PM

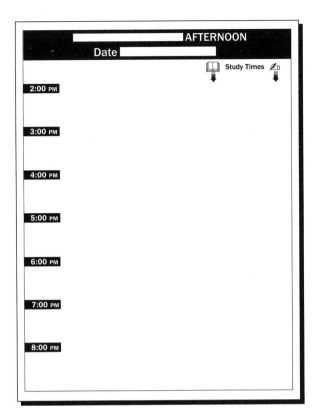

AFTERNOON

Date

Study Times

2:00 PM

3:00 PM

4:00 PM

5:00 PM

6:00 PM

7:00 PM

8:00 PM

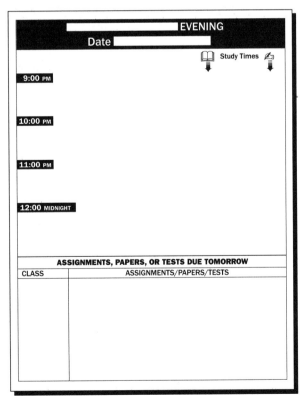

EVENING

Date

Study Times

9:00 PM

10:00 PM

11:00 PM

12:00 MIDNIGHT

ASSIGNMENTS, PAPERS, OR TESTS DUE TOMORROW	
CLASS	ASSIGNMENTS/PAPERS/TESTS

without having to turn the pages. The evening sheet on the next page starts with a block at 9:00 P.M. and continues to midnight.

On the right-hand of each page is a column for your study times. This column appears on all the pages because any time is a good time to study—between classes, during a break at work, while you are eating. These are times you can fit in throughout the day.

At the bottom of the evening page is a section labeled "Assignments/Tests/Papers Due Tomorrow" so that at the end of each day you can look down and see if you have finished that paper, done that assignment, or studied for that test. I recommend filling out this section for each day at the beginning of the week. This section really keeps me on top of things and on my toes. If you are faithful to the calendar and keep it up-to-date, then half of your organization problems will be solved. Be faithful to it and it will be faithful to you.

A STEP-BY-STEP PROCESS FOR MANAGING TIME

Though I developed these steps after many years of trial and error, if you need to alter them to fit your needs, then by all means do so.

Step 1: Make a priority list of what you will be doing in school this semester. For example, Priority 1 should be classes. Priority 2 is study time, and so forth.
Example:
Priority List
1. Classes
2. Study time/tutor time
3. Job
4. Leisure time for sanity
5. Fraternity/sorority meetings, events, sports or other extracurricular activities
6. Volunteer work

Step 2: Set up a calendar for the semester with your courses and course times. In other words, expand on Priority 1.

Step 3: Add your times for studying, Priority 2, to the calendar.

Step 4: Include your activities or obligations on the calendar.

This section is for things other than courses (such as work), or the next priorities you have listed. Continue until you have the whole list on your calendar. You may find that you have to drop some activities to have the time to study and meet with a tutor to get through the semester. To finish my undergraduate and graduate work, I had to cut back on much of my social time. I had to miss many of the events at my school and make some difficult choices about what was important to me.

A Few Tips for Making Up Your Time Schedule:

- ✎ Take advantage of any kind of college orientation before you start your freshman year. In addition, go on a walking tour to help you get familiar with the campus.

- ✎ Plan to do your studying as soon after your classes as possible, as well as during other times, such as waiting for a bus or subway.

- ✎ Schedule breaks in your study time. I find it helpful to study in 50-minute blocks with 10-to-15 minute breaks.

- ✎ Use the list of priorities that you developed to remind you of what you need to be working on.

- ✎ Plan for travel time to and from classes.

Chapter 8

JOY'S TIPS FOR LEARNING HOW TO LEARN

This chapter will probably be the most valuable for you. Many topics will be discussed here, from scheduling and registering for your classes, to getting organized to write a paper. Some of the things that work for me may not work for you. For example, I use color-coding in organizing my papers as well as in my everyday life. If you're color-blind, however, that technique is obviously not going to work for you. Regardless, I urge you to try my strategies if you don't yet have methods of your own—you can always adapt them to work for you.

GETTING STARTED FOR THE SEMESTER: REGISTERING FOR CLASSES

Obviously, your first task is to register for your classes. Registration can be a nightmare. Some colleges have you register for your first classes by mail. If you have this option, be sure that someone looks over your registration form and checks that you have written down the codes correctly. You may have reversed numbers and letters and then find yourself registered for classes you've never heard of.

If registration is done electronically by e-mail, online, or phone, be sure that you punch in the numbers correctly. Sometimes it may take two or three tries to get your whole schedule entered in correctly, especially if you're reading numbers incorrectly and cannot find your mistake. You may be better off going to the Disabled Students Services office and asking one of the staff to punch the numbers in for you. You might also get help from your roommate, if you feel comfortable doing that.

My Experience: My history of attempting to register for classes was marked by many strikeouts. As an undergraduate, I often made mistakes on my registration form. I would copy numbers incorrectly from the semester schedule and/or write the name of the course on the wrong line. At times I even wrote my social security number down wrong by reversing some of the numbers.

Toward the end of my long undergraduate career, when the university I was attending switched to electronic phone registration, I thought the process would be easier for me. After all, I wouldn't have to write. But when I got on that phone and tried to read the numbers off the registration form and then punch them into the system, I was overwhelmed. It was especially hard since I had to do it within a limited amount of time, or I'd have to start all over again.

I finally decided I was going to ask for help registering, so I went to the Disabled Student Services office. They were glad to help me register correctly. I continued to go there to have them do the number punching throughout school. I was amazed at how fast the process can be if you ask for help.

TIPS ON SCHEDULING CLASSES

Here are some tips to help you schedule your classes:

- Do not schedule more classes than you think you can handle in one day. Too much information all at once may overwhelm you.

- Try to sit in on a class before you register for it.

- Register for at least one class each semester in a subject area you find interesting and enjoyable.

KNOWING YOUR STRENGTHS AND CHALLENGES

Part of managing your disability is knowing what you need to get through a class. (This is a tip that will also be helpful in other areas of your life.) Recognizing your strengths and challenges and knowing what accommodations you need is key to your success in post-secondary education.

Weigh your strengths, challenges, and accommodation needs separately for each class of the semester, taking the type of class and its academic requirements into consideration. Start with your strengths. What comes easily to you? How can these assets be transferred to help you in this class? Then move on to your challenges. What is more difficult for you? What has helped you to overcome similar obstacles in the past? Finally, think about what accommodations will help you succeed. These can be accommodations that capitalize on your strengths, such as taking an oral exam if you are skilled at communicating verbally. Or these can be things that diminish your challenges, like being allotted extra time for an exam.

To help you understand your strengths, challenges, and accommodation needs, I've created three worksheets, which appear in Appendix A. Fill out the "strengths" worksheet first, then the "challenges" worksheet, and finally the "accommodations" worksheet.

TALKING TO YOUR PROFESSORS

Going to see your professors before your classes begin will put you ahead of the game. If you are not sure how to break the ice with the professor, then check to see if your school's DSS will send a letter to the professor before you meet. This letter could explain your learning disability and the accommodations you might find helpful. Always ask to see the letter before it is sent, because it **cannot** be sent without your permission.

My Experience: I always appreciated having a letter sent to my professors before the first day of class. I could never think of the right words to start the conversation, so I always start asking the professor about getting a letter from DSS. This question seems to be the right transition into the conversation. However, some instructors have no clue. Once I had a professor who threw me a curve ball. The conversation went like this:

Joy: "Did you get a letter from DSS regarding an LD student? I'm that student."

Physics Professor: "What's LD?"

Needless to say, I was taken aback, but I went on to explain what it was, and he finally recalled a letter he received. Even though the meeting doesn't always go just the way you plan, I find the letter to be really helpful in breaking down that initial barrier between an LD student and the professor.

TAKING EXAMS

Test-taking challenges can vary, depending on the course and the test taker. Your ability to use the methods that I will be discussing will also depend on the support services and resources at your school. But always remember that you have the right to any reasonable accommodations. Several kinds of accommodations can be helpful when you are taking an exam. I urge you to explore all of them and use the ones that best fit your needs and your way of learning.

The first thing to consider is that when you take exams outside of the classroom (i.e., in a room or building different from the one where the class is taking the exam), then the instructor won't be available for questions during the exam. Therefore, meeting and going over the test with the professor should be part of your preparation.

Because you will be taking the exam in a testing room or private office and because you will have extra time, your test will probably be administered by a **proctor.** A proctor is someone who just sits with you while you take a test to make sure that you don't cheat. The proctor is usually provided by the Disabled Student Services office at your college.

A **reader** can also be very helpful in a number of ways. If you do better when you hear the questions or if you must hear as well as follow along on the written exam, you can have a proctor who will read the test questions to you. If so, you will probably be taking the exam in a private testing room so that you don't disturb the rest of the class.

Some professors prefer to read the exam to you themselves, however. Some may even want to read the exam quietly to you in the same room where the class is taking the exam and at the same time. If you don't feel comfortable with this arrangement, let the professor know that having the exam read to you in view of the rest of the class infringes on your right to confidentiality concerning your disability. If the professor insists on being the one to read to you, then you should insist on taking the test in private, either before or after the class takes it.

Scribes help you write the answer down on the exam, and again, this scribe could also be the proctor and reader as well. Many times a professor will suggest a scribe to you if your handwriting is as atrocious as mine. All you do is tell the scribe what to write. This method also helps because you can say the answer out loud and talk yourself through the exam by hearing what you are thinking and using the verbal skills at which LD students often shine. Always have the scribe read the answer back to you. This allows you to hear the answer you gave out loud once more and to make sure he or she wrote what you said.

PCs are also a great idea, and a PC with an adaptive screen device or voice-activated software on it is even better. With it, you don't have to write, and you can print up your legible answers to the test immediately afterward. You may still need someone to read the questions and directions to you. In addition, you should find out if you can run a spell check and/or a grammar program through your answers. Some professors think that somehow answers appear magically on the screen for you, so they won't allow you to use them. But remember, you have a right to whatever reasonable accommodations you need. The definition of "necessary and reasonable" may vary with professors and colleges, however, so you should ask questions about accommodations before you decide to attend the school or take the class.

Oral exams can be another option for those of us who prefer talking through the exam, rather than writing it. This method could work a few different ways. You could have someone read the questions, then you would dictate your answers onto audio tape. After the exam, depending the professor's preference, the office for disabled student services or the professor can transcribe the tape. This type of test taking seems to work really well for those long essay exams.

Another possibility is taking a test orally with the professor. It can be nerve-wracking to tell your answers directly to the instructor, but you don't have to worry about being taped. Only twice in my seven-year undergraduate career did I take an exam this way. The advantage here is really only for the professor, who can usually determine at once whether you studied and know the material and can grade you immediately.

Untimed exams are a given for the student with a learning disability. No matter which of these styles of taking exams you prefer, you should always get double, if not unlimited time to finish an exam. The untimed exam puts no stress on you for a speedy finish. With double time, either you or the proctor still has to keep an eye on the clock. Many times a professor will offer double time just because it's the least that they can do and follow the law. If you are offered only double time, however, and you feel that you need an untimed exam, then by all means fight for it. Explain that processing takes much more time for you than for the average person, as you have to decode and unscramble the information on the test. Let it be known that when you hear the question or read the question, often times you must hear it or read it a second or third time just to understand it or process it in the right order. By no means does this accommodation interfere with the academic integrity of the class or the college or university.

Many of these functions, like proctoring or reading, can be combined. For example, your reader also can act as a proctor and as a scribe. So providing these accommodations is really not a huge expense for a school. Many of the people that do such jobs are the work-study students, who are glad to have a paid job. Of course, if they are being paid by the hour, they prefer that you have ALL the time you need to complete an exam.

WRITING A PAPER: MY COLOR-CODED METHOD

A research paper fills lots of college students with dread. They're afraid to do it and tend to procrastinate about working on it. However, I have a color-coded system that can eliminate some of the grief of organizing and completing this assignment. I call it the color-coded system because I use colored index cards to organize the paper. Here are the steps:

Step 1: Talk to Your Professor

The first step is to discuss possible topics with your professor. Since identifying a topic can be difficult, ask your instructor for suggestions but be sure to pick a topic that interests you. You should have some topics in mind when you meet with your professor. Then you can narrow them down to the one your instructor thinks might best fit the assignment. You may need some help researching the topic, so using your professor as a resource in this area is a good idea, as well.

Keep in mind that the university library is not your only resource. Your school may have a library consortium program that enables you to use books and periodicals from other school libraries. Furthermore, most libraries are connected to a whole network of information via computer. You have all those sources on the Internet to choose from, too.

Step 2: Find Your References

Once you have a clear idea of what you're going to write about, go to the library and begin to look for references by doing a subject search on your topic. You can do this at your college library through the online computer system. Ask the reference librarians for help using these programs.

Don't try to get too many references at one time. Locate about 10 sources and pick the ones most relevant to your subject. This method will help you narrow down to a specific topic. (Remember to use adaptive equipment like the Kurzweil Reader or a tutor to get through your references.) Then locate 10 more sources and keep narrowing those down until you think you have enough to complete your paper. That's all for one day. Take a break and come back to it the next day.

Step 3: Develop an Outline

An outline, if done correctly, can be a real asset in writing your paper. Once you've developed an outline, you've basically written the paper. All you need to do afterward is to fill in any gaps with information from your sources.

The best help for developing an outline is the table of contents from a book on your subject. This page divides the material covered in the book into chapter titles; from these titles you can create entries for your outline.

What follows is an outline based on a paper I wrote on the psychosocial aspects and adjustments for persons with learning disabilities. If you've never done an outline before, you alternate between numbers and letters to organize it, starting by designating the broadest sections as Roman numerals I, II, III, etc. You then subdivide each Roman numeral into capital letters A, B, C, and so forth until you've covered all your subdivisions for that Roman numeral. Each capital letter gets divided into numbers 1, 2, and so on, and each regular number gets divided into small letters a, b, c, etc. The main thing to remember is that you only need to subdivide a section when you have more than one topic to address in that section. In other words, you cannot have a I if you don't eventually expect to have a II; you don't need to create an A if you don't have a B, or a 1 if you don't have a 2.

Although my outline may seem long, it was developed for a graduate-level paper, so I had to make it thorough. Your outline may not be as long or have as many divisions. But it is important that you do an outline correctly—when you have developed a good outline, you will be ready to write your paper.

From here, you're ready to start the color coding. But first take a break.

Psychosocial Aspects and Adjustments for Persons with Learning Disabilities

I. The learning disability
   A. Definition and statistics
   B. Types of learning disabilities
      1. Dyslexia
      2. Dysgraphia
      3. Dyscalcula
      4. Attention-Deficit Disorder(ADD) and Attention-Deficit Hyperactive Disorder(ADHD)
   C. Associated characteristics
      1. Seizure disorder
      2. Motor coordination disorders
         a. Perceptual-motor disorder
         b. Visual-motor disorder
         c. Auditory-motor disorder
      3. Perceptual disorders
         a. Auditory-perceptual disorders
         b. Proprioceptive disorder
         c. Tactile-perceptual disorder
         d. Visual-perceptual disorder
         e. Vestibular-perceptual disorder
      4. Intersensory problems
      5. Memory problems
      6. Soft neurological disorders

II. Assessing and diagnosing the person with a learning disability
   A. Screening and diagnosing techniques and measurements
      1. Basic psycho-educational tests
      2. Other screening techniques
   B. Physical exam
      1. Neurological exam
      2. Behavior assessment
      3. Optical exam

III. Social adjustments of the person with a learning disability
   A. The nonvisible disability
   B. Social status
      1. Acceptance by peers
      2. Social cognition deficits (socially tone deaf) and specific brain hemispheres
         a. Social competencies
         b. Children and adjustment problems
   C. Behavior issues
      1. School avoidance
      2. Homework avoidance
      3. Television addiction
      4. Cheating
      5. Aggression
      6. Controlling behavior
      7. Quitting
      8. Withdrawal
   D. Family issues

IV. Psychological and emotional adjustments of the person with a learning disability
   A. Emotional issues
      1. Self-esteem
      2. Depression and suicide
   B. Personality issues
   C. Drug and alcohol abuse

(continued next page)

(continued from previous page)

V. Treatment
    A. Learning compensations
    B. Developmental optometrists
    C. Special education programs
        1. Within the public school system
        2. Special schools

VI. Learning disabled adults
    A. Employment issues
        1. Protection under the American with Disabilities Act
        2. Disclosure
    B. Social issues
    C. Further education

VII. Implications for the field of vocational rehabilitation and the client with a learning disability
    A. Perceptions of learning disabilities
    B. Learning disabilities and vocational rehabilitation
    C. Self-advocacy
    D. Role models

Step 4: Color Code Your Cards

Once you have a good outline, go back to those sources that you identified and begin finding the information for each section. Assign a color to each Roman numeral division (I, II, III, etc.). Put each bit of information you find on the corresponding colored card.

        I. = white
        II. = blue
        III. = orange

If you can find only white index cards, put a colored dot in the corner of the card with a marker to correspond with the assigned color.

Now you should have index cards of different colors that represent the main sections of your outline (and your paper). Next, put the cards in an envelope or index cardholder. Label this file with a Roman numeral—I or whatever section you're working on. Because the cards are color coded, you will be able to keep them separate. Now take a break.

Step 5: Record More Specific Information

Since an outline gets more specific as you further divide a subject, the next set of cards (A, B, C, etc.) will be a little more specific than the ones for I, II, III, and so on. These will be color-coded the same way as the Roman numeral division cards. For example, if I is white, then IA should be white, too. When you have gone through your references and completed these cards, put them in an envelope and label it with the letter of that division.

After that, you can repeat this process for the next level (1, 2, 3 . . .) and label the envelope "Number 1 information cards."

Repeat the procedure again for the cards with lower-case letters (a, b, c, etc.). Put these in an envelope and label it the same way you did the others. Then you can take a break.

Step 6: Bring All the Pieces Together

At this point, you have gone through your outline and made information cards for every division. For this step you will need a lot of space to spread out all the cards. Begin by opening each envelope, starting with the ones with Roman numerals. Then place the contents of each envelope in a line. Next place the upper-case lettered cards next to the corresponding Roman numeral. Continue this process until you have gone through all the envelopes.

Now you should have a very long line of index cards laid out in the order of your outline. This line may stretch out across your bedroom floor or all the way across a dorm hallway, depending on how comprehensive your paper is. But no matter how long it is, you should realize that you just organized a lot of information in an orderly fashion. So you deserve a long break. (You don't have to leave all the cards on the floor. You can number them and store them in a file box.)

Step 7: Write the Paper

Now you are ready to shape all this information into a well-structured paper. Going card by card, in the order of your outline, write out the information from the cards.

Then take a break.

Step 8: Proofread

Always have an objective person with good writing skills, such as the LD specialist at your school, proofread your paper. Ask that person to read it twice to make sure that the content is easy to follow and that it has no typographical errors. Even today at my job, I have colleagues proofread everything I write. It really makes a difference.

Just a few reminders:

- ✎ Always take advantage of the adaptive equipment available at your school.

- ✎ Ask tutors or note takers to help you in the library.

- ✎ Take as many breaks as you need, even if it is in the middle of a step.

That's my system, and it has worked well for me. But remember, this is a process I discovered that suited the way that I process information. Try it yourself—but don't hesitate to adapt the color-coded method so that it works for you.

TAKING SUMMER COURSES

If you decide to take courses in the summer sessions, you really should know what you're getting into. Summer classes are usually much more accelerated and therefore are harder to keep up with. But not all learning disabled people have problems succeeding in a summer class.

There are many reasons why you may want to take a summer course. For example, you may have failed a course and want to retake it in the summer to be able to graduate on time. Another reason may be to try to finish college a little sooner than your current pace would allow. These are legitimate reasons; however, you should prepare yourself. The following tips should be helpful:

- ✎ Talk to the professor who is teaching the course beforehand. This may be difficult, because many times adjunct professors who are not at the university full-time teach the summer courses. But if you go to the department office, you can probably get the professor's telephone number or leave yours.

✎ Ask questions about the reading load for the class, the number of papers required, the type of exams given, and the length of the term. Summer courses can last anywhere from four to eight weeks.

✎ Tell the professor that you have a learning disability and ask if he or she has ever had an LD student in the summer class before.

✎ Check with your Disabled Student Services office at your school and be sure they know you will be taking a class (or classes). You should also find out if readers and note takers are available for the summer sessions.

✎ Check to see if you can take the course at a community college and transfer the credit to your four-year institution. The benefit is that you may be able to go to your hometown to take the class at the local community college. You may also be able to get more one-to-one attention. If you choose this option, however, be sure that you check with the equivalent department at your full-time college to ensure that they will give you credit for classes you take at another school. The department may wish to see the syllabus or the texts for the course you intend to take, so plan ahead! It is often much more difficult to get approval for courses you've taken at another school after you have taken them.

USING THE STRATEGY PROGRAM

Here are some of my general classroom strategies for success. I think you may find them helpful.

Sit in on a class before you take it.

Tape all lectures.

Review the tapes and transcribe them (or have them transcribed) **as soon after class as possible.**

Arrange in advance for test accommodations and use of adaptive equipment and adaptive methods.

Tutors: Get them and use them. (Preferably tutors who have worked with learning disabled students before.

Every course should be reviewed every day or every other day. Keeping up with the class is vital!

Gauge your time so that you have plenty for studying.

Your own way of learning will help you to succeed.

S **Sitting** in on a class before you register for it is a very wise move. For example, let's say you want to take a chemistry class. If you sit in on it first, you will be able to see how fast the professor talks or how quickly he or she writes things on the board and then erases them. Visiting a class is easy to arrange. All you have to do is go to the professor ahead of time and explain that you are a learning disabled student who is interested in taking the class, but that you want to see if you can handle it before you register. You don't have to identify yourself as a student with a learning disability if you don't want to. You can just be an interested student thinking of taking the class.

Of course, you will have required courses that you have no choice but to take. You will have some flexibility in your electives and your major, however. So when you choose those courses, think back on your testing and the recommendations made to you. Try to emphasize your strengths when you make these decisions. For example, if you have strong verbal skills or if you learn better verbally, why not try a speech class?

T **Taping** all your lectures can be very helpful. For one thing, it is good backup in case your note taker misses something or is absent. Also, taping is invaluable for someone who learns best by repetition. However, as the next tip suggests, playing and replaying your lecture tapes will be of greatest benefit to you if you listen to the tape and study your notes as soon after class as possible.

R **Reviewing** your tapes right after class will help you to remember the material. Your learning disability may make it hard for you to remember information, so before you forget what the class was about, you should listen to that tape.

If you need two modes of input (visual and auditory) to understand what you are reading or listening to, you should have your tapes transcribed. If a reader does your text reading, that person can usually transcribe tapes for you. If not, check with the school's office for disabled student services (or the office that provides services to you), to find out if they can help you make arrangements. Of course, if you can, transcribe the tapes yourself. You may find that the process of transcription helps you to learn the information.

Another form of review I found helpful was something I call conversational learning, something you can do with a study partner or even a tutor. The activity has no special format: you just involve yourself in stimulating discussion about the subject. For example, if you are studying for a religion exam and one of the topics is Catholicism, talking about the power of the Pope or the top three controversies in that religion can help you become familiar with the major focuses of this religion. Then, when you take the essay test, you may remember the words used in that conversation.

A **Accommodations** on tests can vary for each person, and you will need to **arrange** for them in advance. When I was in college, for each exam I had a reader who read me the questions and also wrote down my answers, because most professors found my handwriting very difficult to read. Sometimes a professor would allow me to dictate my answers into a tape recorder. In those cases, the reader only had to read the questions, and then I would put my answers onto the tape. Some professors, however, found it inconvenient to have to listen to a tape. If so, the Office for Disabled Student Services would transcribe the tape before it went to the professor.

T **Tutors** should become a part of your life in college if you are having trouble in a particular area of study. The key is to find a tutor who has worked with people with learning disabilities. The staff at your school's office for disabled student services may be able to recommend an experienced tutor. You may also want to go to the school's education department to find a student in the reading, special education, or teacher training programs who is interested in tutoring. In most of these programs, students work with someone who is learning disabled to fulfill a requirement of their degree.

My Experience: I had a wonderful tutor in the first semester of my graduate program, whom I found through the education department at my university. I had had tutors in my undergraduate career, but they were sometimes impatient and often didn't know how to help me. This tutor was pursuing a master's degree in the reading program and had a special interest in students with learning disabilities. She had tricks to help me broaden my vocabulary, and was a tremendous asset when it came to the grammatical stuff in my papers. My only regret was that I didn't meet her when I was an undergraduate student.

E **Every day** (or every other day) was my rule for reviewing each course. I found that if I started slacking off and I let a course get ahead of me, I would hardly ever catch up. While some people can open a book only in the classroom and still do well on an exam, as a learning disabled person, I am not one of them. I had to work twice as hard to get the same results as other students. It was frustrating, but it was and is still a reality. I know from hard experience that you have to review at least a portion of your notes and tapes from a class and to do it **every day!** Don't get behind!

G **Gauging** your time is a skill you must master. Estimating time is one thing that people with learning disabilities do not do well. A learning disabled student may guess that a task will take an hour, and two hours later she still thinks she has time left over. Frequently, a person with a learning disability will underestimate the time it will take to get from one place to another. Other times, an LD student will plan on finishing something, but before long, the day is gone and he never even started on that paper. Clearly, gauging time correctly is an asset.

I find it helpful to think in blocks of time and use a color-coded calendar like the one described in Chapter 7. One thing you can do is to keep an extra watch in your book bag or tape one to your planner. This practice worked for me on those days when I forgot to wear a watch.

Y The **"YOU"** rule is the last and most important one in my philosophy of learning. The best way to describe what you do in an academic setting (and what you will be doing for the rest of your life) is **learning how to learn.** It is true that because we are learning disabled, we do not succeed as well as others in a traditional learning setting. So, whatever methods you find that help you succeed, use them and stick with them! You must figure out how **you** learn best.

Chapter 9

SUPPORT AND HINTS FOR GENERAL LIVING

SUPPORT

Your emotional well-being is extremely important. It's likely that from time to time, you'll need support from sources outside of yourself, so you need to know where to go for that help. There is a list of resources at the end of this chapter that may assist you. If some of these organizations are not in the area of your school, then call any of the national or international organizations for a local listing of resources or support groups.

First and foremost, however, be aware of groups on campus. For example, your school may have a learning disability resource group or support group. You may want to ask at the Disabled Student Services office or the department that provides your services and accommodations to find out what is available on campus and in the area.

A **support group** may be an informal gathering where LD students get together and just listen to each other. It really helps to talk to someone who knows what you are dealing with every day. You can also hear the horror stories of "fellow sufferers." This exchange can be helpful in identifying the professors and the classes to avoid. If there is not a support group on campus, then go to the disabled student services office and tell them you want to start one. It will really make a difference in your life. At times you will need to vent to those who will best understand exactly what you are going through. Use the help of those disabled students around you.

My Experience: When I was in college I helped start a support group on campus. We would use the group to get information from upperclassmen regarding professors. We would ask which ones were more "disability friendly" and which ones were not. It was sort of a blacklist of professors not to take classes from. I also found out about the good ones—the ones who were more understanding than others. Those are the ones that you want to know about. Their understanding went a long way in helping me get my degrees. If at all possible, avoid the ones who have given other LD students a hard time.

If you can't avoid taking a class with someone you have been warned about, talk to your DSS representative, who probably knows about the professor. Knowing that you have support from that office can help you start the class with a positive attitude and keep it when you encounter a problem. Sometimes your representative can act as a moderator in sticky situations. Always try to work them out, and never burn your bridges—you may have to work with that professor again. Besides the letter that DSS writes, a good way to begin is to let the instructor know that you are taping the class. That way you show respect for the way he or she conducts the course.

The support group was also a source for tips on studying and just getting through college. The group helped to create a network of support in college when I was away from home. It really meant a lot to me and, even today, the people from that original group are still my close friends.

A **resource group,** by contrast, is one that schedules speakers and workshops. More of an informational group than the support group, the resource group may be especially helpful to the LD college student who is not aware of certain services, technology, and other things that will help make the semester a little bit easier. Some groups may also combine resources and support.

The **career center** is another good resource. They may offer informative speakers or workshops.

Frequently, the career center on campus has support groups, as well.

Within the college, your **academic advisor** can be a valuable resource. Use this person for advice on your class schedule. You should also be aware that your **advisor at Disabled Students Services** or your **learning disabilities specialist** may act as a liaison between you and your academic advisor, especially if your advisor has not worked with a student who has a learning disability before.

If you find yourself becoming overwhelmed or depressed, another person who can help is a **counselor.** Consult your college counseling center for a referral. Counseling can be an essential part of your semester. Don't hesitate to use this service if you need to.

My Experience: I have been and always will be an advocate of counseling. At times I was overwhelmed by frustrations with school, on top of other events in my life, and seeing a mental health professional was the solution for me. The process worked, and I got through some hard times. I realized that I had put in too much work to let some emotional issues go unattended and ruin my chances of accomplishing my goals.

If you are on medication for ADHD, then continue to communicate with your physician. This communication is imperative, because your medication doses may need to be adjusted from time to time.

THE VOCATIONAL REHABILITATION COUNSELOR

A vocational rehabilitation counselor is one of the best resources I can recommend to you. As a disabled person, you are entitled to the services offered by your state vocational rehabilitation services. These are the offices in every state that offer vocational rehabilitation services to persons with disabilities. If you have an IEP in place in your school now, then chances are that you have had a vocational rehabilitation counselor on your IEP transition team since your junior year in high school.

The office of vocational rehabilitation services offers a variety of services to disabled persons, including assessment, diagnostic services, vocational training, job placement, and reimbursement for certain accommodation items if that accommodation will lead to gainful employment. These professionals also provide career counseling and vocational evaluation, if needed. Some states have vocational rehabilitation centers that allow clients to try different types of assistive technology. And all of these services are FREE. This program has helped put disabled persons into training and work since 1973.

If you do not have a vocational counselor on your IEP team, then you should make an appointment with your local vocational rehabilitation office and get in the system. You can find them listed under the government pages in your local phone book. Your school may also assist you in getting registered. If you are already planning to go away to college, you should register now with your vocational rehabilitation office in your state of residence. Your assigned vocational counselor will help you prepare for this very important transition to college. You will determine your counselor's level of involvement.

Once you go there, all of your current documentation will be assessed, but you may be asked to take more tests and get more assessments. If you have enough and you are found to be eligible for services, then you will begin working on an "individual employment plan," because the goal of the vocational rehabilitation counselor is to place you in substantial gainful employment. This plan will include the steps that it takes to get you to the goal. For example, if your goal is to become a speech therapist and you will need a bachelor's degree to reach that goal, then that degree is what vocational rehabilitation will pay for. Your college degree is the training you need to reach your stated employment goal.

My Experience: I finally registered with vocational rehabilitation after I had already spent a few years in college. I found out about it from another student I met who told me that her state VR was paying for her tuition. In my case, the VR covered more testing because I had a few other medical issues directly related to my disability. The VR also paid for a developmental optometrist who provided me with eye training and a pair of special glasses to help me read. Finally, the VR covered my medication. All of these elements were impairment-related expenses that I needed to reach my stated employment goal. As long as everything was directly related to my goal, it was considered a reasonable expense.

The vocational rehabilitation counselor is going to be one the best supports that you can have as you work toward your stated goal.

GENERAL LIVING TIPS

Since life in general gives me headaches, I find that the less complicated I make my life, the better off I am.

Money

For example, I have problems with money. Figuring how much change I should get back after I make a purchase has always been hard for me. I had to find a way to avoid this headache, at least some of the time. The answer was the **meal card** that most colleges have. At the beginning of each month, you put the amount of money you think you'll need to pay for food on the card. This way, the amount you spend for each meal is subtracted from the card. You have no change to worry about, just the card. Presto, here was one less headache!

Another major headache I had with money was reconciling my account at the end of the month because the columns are so small, and I had a hard time staying in the columns in the **checkbook register**. My solution was to use color-coding with my checking account. There are several ways to do this, so you need to find what works for you. I color-code the spending/withdrawals and the deposits. All money coming in is in GREEN. All money going out is in RED. I also write the monthly bills that come up every month in BLUE. At a glance, if I want to know how much money I have for spending, I know right away because I can see the minimum for bills that I need each month.

Manage Your Time

Another obvious tip is time management control. Use the LD calendar. It will make all the difference in the world. Make a schedule that allows for study time and leisure time. Make room for upcoming papers and the research time you will need to get them done. If you block the time into your calendar then you are more likely to make sure you get it done. You must have complete control over your own time. If you do not, then it will take control of you. USE THE CALENDAR! It will make a difference. Time management should also allow for a social life—well, some social life. Be good to yourself in this regard, but not too good.

Living Environment

Your living environment will be very important to your success. Be prepared for those roommates who are not easy to study around and who don't have time management skills that allow you the study time that you need. It will be up to you to be assertive and make clear that you need some quiet time and a quiet place where you can study if your own room is a problem.

Know Your Needs

Know your disability. Know all about your strengths and challenges. Know how to describe your disability to everyone who needs to know about it to make your college experience a successful one.

Educate, advocate, and disclose are the three rules to live by. If you do not educate people about your disability, no one else will. If you do not advocate for yourself, there will be days when no one else will. If you do not disclose your disability, then no one will know that you need accommodations. College or university administrators and the professors are not mind readers. You must be able to ask for what you need, and therefore, you must disclose what your challenges are.

Persevere!

Use this book as a guide for creating your own strategies and survival methods. You can be and accomplish anything you want to. There are learning disabled professionals all over the world in every career imaginable. Don't settle on the field or career that is an easy way out. You will always be learning how to learn, no matter what path you choose, and good is not enough when you dream of being great!

AFTERWORD

Please let me hear about your experiences. I really do want to find out about your learning disability and your college experience. Anything that you find useful may be useful to others. Please send your comments, stories, and tips to:

Learning How to Learn
147 North French Street
Alexandria, VA 22304
Fax: 703/823-8349
joycobb@learninghowtolearn.org
www.learninghowtolearn.org

Appendix A

WORKSHEETS AND OTHER HELPFUL TOOLS

CHECKLIST OF QUESTIONS TO ASK AT COLLEGES AND UNIVERSITIES

(From Chapter 5, pp. 35–43.)

College _____ **Telephone** _____

Contact person _____

QUESTIONS TO ASK	YES	NO
Does this college or university have a learning disabilities program, or does it provide services for the learning disabled under general disabled services? — Learning disability program or structured program — Learning disability services		
If the college or university has a separate LD program, do I need to apply to that program as well as to the college?		
What documentation of my learning disability does this college require ? _____ _____		
Does the college or university have an added fee for use of the services for the learning disabled?		
Does the college or university provide any of the following accommodations: — Test proctors — Extended time on exams — Option for oral exams — Note takers — Tape recorders in classes — Tutorial help specifically for LD students — Textbooks on tape or readers for textbooks		
Does the college or university have equipment that can assist the learning disabled?		
What specific equipment does the college or university have? — Kurzweil Reader — Dictation software (Brand) _____ — (Other) _____		
Does this college provide curriculum modification?		
Does the college provide the option of completing a four-year degree program in five years or longer?		
Does the college or university have an LD support or resource group?		

NOTES:

MORNING

Date _____

📖 **Study Times** ✍️

7:00 AM

8:00 AM

9:00 AM

10:00 AM

11:00 AM

12:00 NOON

1:00 PM

Study Times

2:00 PM

3:00 PM

4:00 PM

5:00 PM

6:00 PM

7:00 PM

8:00 PM

9:00 PM

	EVENING
Date	

Study Times

9:00 PM

10:00 PM

11:00 PM

12:00 MIDNIGHT

ASSIGNMENTS, PAPERS, OR TESTS DUE TOMORROW

CLASS	ASSIGNMENTS/PAPERS/TESTS

NOTES:

WORKSHEET 1: WHAT ARE MY STRENGTHS?

"The beauty of the desert is that somewhere lies a well."

(From Chapter 8, p. 73.)

What things do I find easy to do? What things do I excel in? What things can I help others with?

Examples: I am able to speak well in front of a group.

I do well working on a project in a group.

I am able to show others how to work with tools.

I can learn computer programs very easily.

_____

_____

_____

_____

_____

_____

_____

_____

_____

_____

_____

_____

_____

_____

_____

_____

Tip: After you have your strengths down, think about how those activities are transferable to other areas. For example, if you speak well in front of a group, perhaps you can take oral exams.

Worksheet 2: WHAT ARE MY CHALLENGES?

"We are all just pilgrims on the same journey...but some pilgrims have better road maps." – Nelson DeMille

(From Chapter 8, p. 73)

What do I find difficult to do? What do I need help with most of the time? What things do I get help with or get accommodations for?

Examples: I have difficulty reading and writing numbers.

I have difficulty taking notes and listening at the same time.

I always need more time to complete a written task than most people do.

I have a difficult time organizing the work once I complete it.

_____

_____

_____

_____

_____

_____

_____

_____

_____

_____

_____

_____

Tip: After you have written down your challenges, try to think of what things you have done in the past to make these tasks easier. These things may be the accommodations you will need for your college classes.

WORKSHEET 3: ACCOMMODATIONS

"In order to ask for help, I need to know what my needs are."

(From Chapter 8, p. 73)

What do I need to make to the playing field level? What works for me in school or at work? What special needs or conditions do I require to get through my day?

Examples: I need a reader for test.

I need a distraction-free environment.

I need a list that I can check off as I do each task that is expected of me.

I need to color code files and paperwork such as study notes.

_____

_____

_____

_____

_____

_____

_____

_____

_____

_____

_____

_____

_____

_____

Tip: Fill out all three worksheets for each class, taking into account the academic requirements for each class.

Appendix B

SCHOOLS WITH EXTENSIVE LD SERVICES

The following colleges and universities are ones that I rate as the top ones in the country for LD students. My criteria are these:

- ✎ The school has a learning disabilities specialist available to students

- ✎ The school has a Kurzweil Reader or other adaptive technology available to students

- ✎ The school has readers to put texts on tape if the book is not available through Recordings for the Blind & Dyslexic.

A If a school meets all of the criteria listed above, then it is a Class A school.

B If a school meets two of the criteria listed above, then it is a Class B school.

C If a school meets one of the criteria listed above, then it is a Class C school.

**A$** If a school meets all of the criteria listed above, but there are extra costs involved, then it is a Class A$ school.

Alabama

University of Alabama
Jim Saski, Office of Disabilities
Tuscaloosa, AL
205/348-5175

Alaska

University of Alaska
Lyn Stoller, Disability Support Services
Anchorage, AK
907/786-4530

Sheldon Jackson University
Alice Smith, Learning Assistance Program
Sitka, AK
907/747-5235

Arizona

A Arizona State University
Tedde Scharf, Disabled Students Resources
Tempe, AZ 85287
408/965-1234

A Northern Arizona University
Marsha Fields, Disability Support Services
Flagstaff, AZ
520/523-8773

B University of Arizona
Diane C. Perreira, Strategic Alternate
  Learning Techniques
Tucson, AZ
520/621-1327

Arkansas

A Harding University
Linda Thompson, Student Support
  Services Searcy
Searcy, AR
501/279-4416

A$ University of the Ozarks
Julia Frost, Jones Learning Center
Clarksville, AR
501/979-1401

California

A Bakersfield College
Tim Bohan, Support Services Program
Bakersfield, CA
805/395-4520

B California Polytechnical State University
(also has LD newsletter)
John Hanna, Disability Resource Center
San Luis Obispo, CA
805/756-1395

B San Francisco State University
Kimberly Bartlett, PhD, Disability
Resource Center
San Francisco, CA
415/338-2472

C Santa Clara University
Alexa Varby, Students with Disabilities
  Resources
Santa Clara, CA
408/554-4109

B Sierra College
Dr. James Hirschinger, Learning
  Opportunities Center
Rocklin, CA
707/664-2505

C Sonoma State University
Linda Lipps, Disability Resource Center
Rohnert Park, CA
916/781-0599

A Stanford University
Joan Bisagno, PhD, Disability Resource
  Center
San Jose, CA
650/723-1066

A University of California (Berkeley)
Connie Chiba, Disabled Students
  Program
Berkeley, CA
510/642-0518

A University of California (Santa Barbara)
Diane Glenn, Disabled Student Program
Santa Barbara, CA
805/893-2182

Colorado

B University of Colorado (Boulder)
Terri Bodhaine, Disability Services
Boulder, CO
303/492-5601

Connecticut

B Fairfield University
Rev. W. Lawrence O'Neil, Student
    Support Service
Fairfield, CT
203/254-4000

B University of Hartford
Marcia Gilder Orcutt, Learning Plus
West Hartford, CT
860/768-4522

B Mitchell College
Patricia Pezzullo, Learning Resource Center
New London, CT
860/701-5141

District of Columbia

A$ American University
Helen Steinberg, Learning Services Program
Washington, DC
202/885-3360

A The Catholic University
Barbara Bernhardt, Multicultural and
    Special Services
Washington, DC
202/319-5126

A University of the Pacific
Vivian Snyder, Office of Learning
    Disability Support
Stockton, CA 95211
209/946-3218

B University of Southern Colorado
Peter Bouchard, Disability Services Office
Pueblo, CO
719/549-2581

A Southern Conn. State University
Suzanne Tucker, Disability Resource Office
New Haven, CT
203/392-6828

A University of Connecticut
Joan McGuire, University Program for LD
    Students
Storrs, CT
860/486-0178

A The George Washington University
Christy Willis, Disabled Student Services
Washington, DC
202/994-8250

Florida

 Barry University
Jill Reed, Center for Advanced Learning
Miami Shores, FL
305/899-3485

 Florida A & M University
Sharon M. Wooten, Learning
Development and Evaluation Center
Tallahassee, FL
850/599-8474

Georgia

 Brenau University
Vincent Yamilkoski, Learning Center
Gainesville, GA
770/534-6124

 Emory University
Tricia Jacob, Disability Services
Atlanta, GA
404/727-6016

Idaho

 University of Idaho
Meredeth L. Goodwin, Student Support
Services
Moscow, ID
208/885-6746

Illinois

B DePaul University
Karen D. Wold, Director Productive
Learning Strategies (PLUS Program)
Chicago, IL
773/325-4239

B Florida Atlantic University
Beverly Warde, Director Office for
Students with Disabilities (OSD)
Boca Raton, FL
561/297-3880

University of Florida
James Costello, Services for Students
with Disabilities
Gainesville, FL
352/392-1261

A Georgia State University
Caroline Gergly, Disability Services
Atlanta, GA
404/463-9044

A$ University of Georgia
Noel Gregg, Learning Disabilities Center
Athens, GA
706/542-4589

A Illinois State University
Ann M. Caldwell, Disability Concerns
Normal, IL
309/438-5853

B Kendall College
Michelle Sinka, Freshman Program
Evanston, IL
847/866-1300 X-1387

C Lincoln College
Pat Burke, Supportive Educational Services
Lincoln, IL
800/569-556

B National-Louis University
Anna Hammond, Services for Students
with Special Needs
Evanston, IL
847/475-1100

C Northern Illinois University
Nancy Kasinsky, Center for Access-
Ability Resources (CAAR)
DeKalb, IL
815/753-1303

Indiana

B Anderson University
Rinda Vogelgesang, Office for Disabled
Student Services
Anderson, IN
800/428-6414 or 765/641-4226

C Ball State University
Richard Harris, Disabled Student
Development
Muncie, IN
765/285-5293

A Indiana University
Lynn Flinders, Office of Disabled Students
Bloomington, IN
812/855-3508

A Northwestern University
Matthew Tominey, Services for Students
with Disabilities
847/467-5530

A$ Southern Illinois University
Barbara Cordoni, Disability Support
Services & Achieve Program
Carbondale, IL
618/453-5738

A University of Illinois (Urbana-Champaign)
Brad Hedrick, Division of Rehabilitation/
Ed. Services
Urbana, IL
217/333-4600

B Manchester College
Denise L. S. Howe, Services for
Students with Disabilities
Manchester, IN
219/982-5076

A$ University of Indianapolis
Deborah Spinney, B.U.I.L.D.
Indianapolis, IN
800/232-8634 or 317/788-3536

Iowa

 Cornell College
Joan Caar, Student Services
Vernon, IA
319/895-4234

 Loras College
Dianne Gibson, Learning Disabilities
  Program
Dubuque, IA 52001
800/245-6727 or 319/588-7134

Kansas

 Kansas State University
Gretchen Holden, Disabled Student
  Services
Manhattan, KS
785/532-6441

Kentucky

 Eastern Kentucky University
Teresa Bellusio, Project SUCCESS
Richmond, KY
606/622-1500

Louisiana

 Louisiana State University
Traci Bryant, Office of Disability Services
Baton Rouge, LA
225/334-2652

Maine

 Unity College
James Horan, Student Support Services
Unity, ME
207/948-3131

 Saint Ambrose University
Gary Buckley, Services for Students with
  Disabilities
Davenport, IA
319/333-6275

 University of Iowa
Mary Richard, Student Disability Services
Iowa City, IA 52242
319/335-1462

 University of Kansas
Lorna Zimmer, Services for Students
  with Disabilities
Lawrence, KS
785/864-4064

 University of New Orleans
Janice Lyn, PhD, Disabled Student Services
New Orleans, LA
504/280-6222

University of New England
Carolyn Ehringhaus, Individual Learning
  Program (ILP)
Biddeford, ME
207/283-0171 X-2561

Maryland

B Frostburg State University
Leroy Pullen, Disability Support Services
Frostburg, MD
301/687-4483

A$ McDaniel College
(formerly Western Maryland College)
Denise Marjarun, Academic Skills Center
410/857-2504

Massachusetts

A$ American International College
Mary Saltus, Supportive Learning Services
for Learning Disabled Students
Springfield, MA
413/747-6426

A$ Boston University
Lorraine Wolf, Learning Disabilities
Support Services
Boston, MA 02215
617/353-3658

A$ Bradford College
Barbara Sherbody, College Learning
Haverhill, MA
978/372-7161

B Clark University
Alan Bier, Disability Service
Worcester, MA
508/793-7468

A$ Curry College
Lisa Ijiri, Director, Program for
Advancement for Learning (PAL)
Milton, MA
617/333-0500

C Towson State University
Veronica (Ronnie) Uhland, Disability
Support Services
Towson, MD
410/830-2638

C University of Maryland
William Scales, Disability Support Services
College Park, MD
301/314-7682

A$ Dean College
Kevin Kelly, Personalized Learning Services
Franklin, MA
508/541-1508

A$ Mount Ida College
Jill Mehler, Learning Opportunities Program
Newton Centre, MA
617/928-4648

A$ Northeastern University
Dean Ruth Bork, Disability Resource
Center
Boston, MA
617/337-2675

B Pine Major College
Mary Walsh, Learning Resource Center
Chestnut Hill, MA
800/762-1357

A University of Massachusetts (Amherst)
Patricia Gillespi- Silver, Learning
Disability Support Services
Amherst, MA
413/545-4602

Michigan

A Adrian College
Jane McCloskey, Project EXCEL
Adrian, MI
517/265-5161

A Aquinas College
Gary Kieff, Academic Achievement
   Center
Grand Rapids, MI
616/459-8281

B Calvin College
James Mackenzie, Student Academic
   Services
Grand Rapids, MI
616/957-6113

B Ferris State University
Eunice Merwin, Disabilities Services
Grand Rapids, MI
616/592-3772

Minnesota

A Augsburg College
Susan Carlson, Center for Learning and
   Adaptive Student Services
Minneapolis, MN
612/330-1648

C Moorhead State University
Paula Ahles, Disability Services
Moorhead, MN
218/299-5859

C St. Olaf College
Linda Hunter, Academic Support Center
Northfield, MN
507/646-3288

A Michigan State University
Margaret Chmielewski,
   Disability Resource Center
East Lansing, MI
517/353-9642

A University of Michigan
Stuart Segal, Services for Students with
   Disabilities
Ann Arbor, MI
734/763-3000

A Northern Michigan University
Lynn Walden, Disability Services
Marquette, MI
906/227-1550

A Suomi College
Carol Bates, Learning Disabilities Program
Hancock, MI
906/487-7258

B University of Minnesota (Duluth)
Penny Cragus, Learning Disabilities
   Program
Duluth, MN
218/726-7965

A University of Minnesota
Bobbi Cordano, Disability services
Minneapolis, MN 55455-0213
612/624-4120

Mississippi

 University of Southern Mississippi
Valerie DeCoux, Ph.D., Office of Services
  for Students with Disabilities
Hattiesburg, MS
601/266-5756

Missouri

 Kansas City Art Institute
Mary Manger, Academic Resource
  Center
Kansas City, MO
816/ 472-4852

A$ Southwest Missouri State University
Steve Capps, Learning Diagnostic Clinic
417/ 836-4787

B University of Missouri
Sarah Colby Weaver, Disability Services
Columbia, MO
573/ 882-4696

C Washington University
Fran Lang, Disability Resource Center
St. Louis, MO 63130-4899
314/ 935-4062

A$ Westminster College
Hank F. Ottinger, Learning Disabilities
  Program
Fulton, MO 65251
573/592-5305

Montana

 University of Montana
James Marks, Disability Services for
  Students
Missoula, MT
406/243-2373

C Northern Montana College
John Donaldson, Student Support
  Services
Havre, MT
406/ 265-3783

A Rocky Mountain College
Jane Van Dyke, Services for Academic
  Success
Billings, MT
406/ 657-1128

Nevada

 Truckee Meadows Community College
Harry Heiser, Student Support Services
Reno, NV
702/ 673-7286

New Hampshire

 Colby-Sawyer College
Mary Mar, Academic Development Center
New London, NH
603/526-3714

 New England College
Anna Carlson, Academic Advising and
   Support Center
Henniker, NH
603/428-2218

 New Hampshire College
Richard Colfer, the Learning Center
Manchester, NH
603/ 645-9606

 Notre Dame College
Jane O'Neil, Learning Enrichment Center
Manchester, NH
603/669-4294

 University of New Hampshire
Margo W. Druschel, ACCESS
Durham, NH
603/862-2607

New Jersey

 Fairleigh Dickinson University
Mary Farrell, Regional Center for College
   Students with Learning Disabilities
Rutherford, NJ
201/692-2087

Kean University
Marie Segal, Project Excel
Union, NJ
908/527-2380

 Monmouth University
Anne Grad, Support for Students with
   Disabilities
West Long Branch, NJ
732/ 571-3460

 Rider University
Jacqueline Simon, Education
   Enhancement Program
Lawrenceville, NJ
609/ 896-5241

Seton Hall University
Raynette Gardner, Student Support
   Services
South Orange, NJ
973/761-9166

New Mexico

B New Mexico State University
Jane Spinti, Services for Students with
Disabilities
Las Cruces, NM
505/ 646-6840

New York

A$ Adelphi University
Susan Spencer, Learning Disabled
College Students
Garden City, NY 11530
516/877-4710

B Colgate University
Lynn Waldman, Academic Program Support
Hamilton, NY
315/824-7225

A Cornell University
Disability Services, Office of Equal Opportunity
Ithaca, NY
607/255-3976

A$ Hofstra University
Ignacio Gotz, Program for Academic
Learning Skills (PALS)
Hemstead, NY
516/463-5841

A$ Iona College
Madeline Packerman, College
Assistance Program (CAP)
New Rochelle, NY
914/633-2582

A$ Long Island University-C. W. Post College
Carol Rundlett, Academic Resource
Center (ARC)
Brookville, NY
516/299-2937

B Manhattan College
Ross Pollack, Learning Disabilities Program
Riverdale, NY
718/862-7101

A$ Marist College
Linda Cooper Office of Special Services,
Learning Disabilities Program
Poughkeepsie, NY
914/575-3274

A New York University
Alexandra Klein, Access To Learning
New York, NY
212/ 998-4980

A Rochester Institute of Technology
Carla Katz, Learning Support Services
Rochester, NY 14623
716/475-5296

B Saint Bonaventure University
Debra A. Bookmiller, Services for
Students with Disabilities
Bonaventure, NY
716/375-2066

A SUNY College of Technology (Alfred)
Jeanne Mead, Services for Students
With Disabilities
607/ 587-3112

C State University of New York (Farmingdale)
Malka Edelman, Support Services for
  Students with Disabilities
516/420-2311

B State University of New York (Potsdam)
Tamara Durant, Accommodative Services
Potsdam, NY
315/267-3267

B St. Lawrence University
John Meagher, Office of Special Needs
Canton, NY
315/229-5104

North Carolina

C Appalachian State University
Arlene Lundquist, Learning Disability
  Program
Boone, NC
704/262-2291

B Duke University
Kathryn Gustafson, Ph. D., Services for
  Students with Disabilities
Durham, NC
919/ 684-5917

C East Carolina University
C. C. Rowe, Department for Disability
  Support
Greenville, NC 27858-4353
252/328-6799

B Guilford College
Sue Keith, Academic Skills Center
Greensboro, NC
336/ 316-2200

A University of North Carolina (Chapel Hill)
Jane Byron, Learning Disabilities Services
Chapel Hill, NC
919/ 962-7227

A$ St. Thomas Aquinas College
Erica Warren, The "STAC" Exchange
Sparkill, NY
914/398-4230

A Syracuse University
James Duah-Agyeman, Learning
  Disability Services
Syracuse, NY 13244
315/443-3976

B University of North Carolina (Charlotte)
Janet L. Filer, Disability Services
Charlotte, NC
704/547-4355

A University of North Carolina (Wilmington)
Peggy Turner, Disability Services
Wilmington, NC
910/962-3746

C Wake Forest University
Van D. Westerfelt, Learning Assistance
  Center
Winston- Salem, NC
336/ 759-5929

B Western Carolina University
Carol Mellon, Disability Student Services
Cullowhee, NC
828/227-7234

A$ Wingate College
Linda Stedje-Larson, Specific Learning
  Disabilities
Wingate, NC
704/233-8269

North Dakota

B North Dakota State College of Science
Rene Moen, Study Services for Students
  with Disabilities
Wahpeton, ND
701/671-2335

A North Dakota State University
Catherine Anderson, Disability Services
Fargo, ND
701/231-7671

Ohio

A Central Ohio Technical College
Phyllis E. Thomson, Ph.D, Disability
  Services
Newark, OH
740/366-9246

A Hocking College
Elaine Dabeklo Access Center
Nelsonville, OH
740/753-1452

A Kent State University
Anne Jannarone, Student Disability
  Services
Kent, OH
330/ 672-3391

A Miami University
Lois Phillips, Learning Disabilities Program
Oxford, OH
513/ 529-8799

A$ Muskingum College
Amy Butts, PLUS Program
New Concord, OH 43762
740/826-8137

A Oberlin College
Dean Kelly, Ph.D., Office of Services for
  Students with Disabilities
Oberlin, OH
440/775-8461

B Ohio University
Katherine Fahay, Office for Institutional
  Equity/ Disability Student Services
Athens, OH
740/ 593-2620

C University of Cincinnati
Debra Merchant, Disability Services
Cincinnati, OH 45221-009
513/556-6823

C University of Toledo
Kendra Johnson, Office of Accessibility
Toledo, OH
419/ 530-4981

A$ Ursuline College
Cynthia Russell, Program for Students
  with LD
Pepper Pike, OH
440/ 646-8318

Oklahoma

 University of Oklahoma
Suzette Dyer, Office of Disability Services
Norman, OK
405/325-3163

Oregon

 Oregon State University
Tracey Bentley-Townlin, Services For
Students with Disabilities
Corvallis, OR
541/737-4098

 Western Oregon University
Martha R. Smith, Office of Disability
Services
Monmouth, OR
503/838-8250

Pennsylvania

 Clarion University of Pennsylvania
Gregory K. Clary, Student Support Services
Clarion, PA
814/226-2347

 Gannon University
Sister Joyce Lowery, Program for
Students with Learning Disabilities
Erie, PA
814/871-5326

College Misericordia
Joseph Rogan, Alternative Learners Project
Dallas, PA
717/674-6347

 Kutztown University of Pennsylvania
Barbara N. Peters, Services for Students
with Disabilities
Kutztown, PA
610/683-4108

Drexel University
Bill Welsh, Office of Disability Services
Philadelphia, PA
215/895-2507

 Mercyhurst College
Barbara Weigert, Program for Students
with Learning Differences
Erie, PA
814/824-2450

East Stroudsburg University of Pennsylvania
Edith F. Miller, Disability Services
East Stroudsburg, PA 18301-2999
570/422-3825

Pennsylvania State University
(University Park)
Deborah Merchant, Learning Disabilities
Support Services
University Park, PA
814/863-1807

 Edinboro University of Pennsylvania
Robert McConnell, Office for Students
with Disabilities (OSD)
Edinboro, PA
814/732-2462

University of Pittsburgh
Marcie Roberts, Disability Support
  Services
Pittsburgh, PA
412/648-7890

Rhode Island

 Brown University
Susan Pilner, Students with Alternative
  Learning Styles
Providence, RI
401/ 863-2378

B Johnson and Whales University
Meryl Berstein, Student
  Success/Special Needs
Providence, RI
401/598-4689

South Carolina

 University of South Carolina (Columbia)
Joyce Haddock, Academic Support Services
Columbia, SC
803/ 777-6142

South Dakota

 Black Hills State University
Sharon Hemmingson, Student Support
  Services
Spearfish, SD
605/ 642-6099

A Northern State University
Paul Kraft, Learning Center
Aberdeen, SD
605/626-2371

 Temple University
Dorothy M. Cobula, Disability Resources
  and Services
Philadelphia, PA
215/ 204-1280

A Providence College
Rose A. Boyle, Office of Academic
  Services
Providence, RI
401/865-1219

C South Dakota State University
Eugene Butler, Jr., Disabled Student
  Services
Brookings, SD
605/688-4496

Tennessee

B
Lee University
Susan Sasse, Academic Support Program
Cleveland, TN
423/614-8181

A$
University of Tennessee at Chattanooga
Debra Anderson, College Access Program
Chattanooga, TN
423/755-4006

A$
University of Tennessee (Martin)
Barbara Gregory, Program Access for
College
Martin, TN
901/587-7195

Texas

A
Abiline Christian University
Gloria Bradshaw, Alpha Academic Services
Abiline, TX
915/674-2750

C
Lamar University
Callie Trahan, Services for Students with
Disabilities
Beaumont, TX
409/880-8026

B
Southern Methodist University
Rebecca Marin, Services For Students
with Disabilities
Dallas, TX
214/ 768-4563

B
Southwestern Texas State University
Tina Schultz, Office of Disability Services
San Marcos, TX
512/245-3451

B
Texas A&M University
Anne Reber, Students with Disabilities
College Station, TX
409/458-1214

A
University of Houston
Raina Dass, Center for Students with
Disabilities
Houston, TX
713/743-5400

A
University of North Texas
Steve Pickett, Office of Disability
Accommodations
Denton, TX
940/565-4323

B
University of Texas (El Paso)
Susan J. Lopez, Disabled Student
Services
El Paso, TX
915/747-8712

Utah

B
Brigham Young University
Paul Boyd, Services to Students with
Learning Disabilities
Provo, UT
801/378-2767

B
Southern Utah University
Lynne J. Brown, Student Support Services
Cedar City, UT
435/586-7771

A Utah State University
Diane Craig Baum, Disability Resource
    Center
Logan, UT
435/797-2444

Vermont

C Champlain College
Becky Peterson, Support Services for
    Students
Burlington, VT
802/ 860-2700

B Johnson State College
Katherine Veileux, Academic Support
    Services
Johnson, VT
802/ 635-1259

C Landmark College
MacLean Gander, Landmark College
Putney, VT
802/ 387-4767

Virginia

B George Mason University
Paul Bousel, Disability Support Services
Fairfax, VA
703/ 993-2474

B James Madison University
Louis Hedrick, Office of Disability Services
Harrisburg, VA
540/ 568-6705

A Old Dominion University
Dr. Nancy Oltnoff, Disability Services
Norfolk, VA
757/683-4655

B Norwich University
Paula A. Gills, Learning Support Center
(LSC)
Northfield, VT
802/485-2130

B Southern Vermont College
Linda Crowe, Disabilities Support
Program
Bennington, VT
802/442-6360

A University of Vermont
Nancy Oliker, Office of Specialized
Student Services
Burlington, VT
802/656-7753

A University of Virginia
Scott Parker, Learning Needs &
Evaluation Center (LNEC)
Charlottesville, VA
804/243-5180

A Virginia Intermont College
Talmage Dobbins, Student Support
    Services
Bristol, VA
540/669-6101

Washington

 Washington State University
Marshall Mitchell, Disability Resource
Center
Pullman, WA
509/335-1726

 Eastern Washington University
Karen Raver, Disability Support Services
Cheney, WA
509/359-6871

West Virginia

 Marshall University
Barbara P. Guyer, Higher Education for
Learning Problems (HELP)
Huntington, WV
304/696-6317

West Virginia Wesleyan College
Shirley Fortney, Special Support Services
Buckhannon, WV
304/473-8380

Wisconsin

Alverno College
Nancy Bornstein, Instructional Services
Center
Milwaukee, WI
414/382-6353

University of Wisconsin (Madison)
J. Trey Duffy, McBourney Disability
Resource Center
Madison, WI
608/263-2741

University of Wisconsin (Eau-Clair)
Joseph C. Hisrich, Services for Students
with Disabilities (SSD)
Eau Claire, WI
715/836-4542

University of Wisconsin (Milwaukee)
Vicki Groser, Learning Disabilities
Program
Milwaukee, WI
414/ 229-6239

University of Wisconsin (LaCrosse)
June Reihert, Disability Resource
Services
LaCrosse, WI
608/785-6900

University of Wisconsin (Stevens Point)
John Timack, Office of Disability
Services
Stevens Point, WI
715/346-3365

Wyoming

University of Wyoming
Chris Primus, University Disability
Support Services
Laramie, WY
307/766-6189

Appendix C

RESOURCES

ORGANIZATIONS THAT PROVIDE SERVICES AND PRODUCTS FOR THE LEARNING DISABLED

Children and Adults with Attention Deficit Disorder (CHADD)

CHADD is an organization that offers support for those who are dealing with Attention Deficit Disorder. The CHADD National Call Center (Monday to Friday, 8:15 A.M.–5:15 P.M. EST) offers Information and Referral services. The website offers a lot of information about education and employment needs. This is a thorough information source.

800/233-4050 (National Call Center)

http://www.chadd.org

Council for Learning Disabilities (CLD)

P. O. Box 40303
Overland Park, KS 62204
913/492-8755

ERIC Clearinghouse on Adult, Career, and Vocational Education

A clearinghouse with 24-hour voice mail service providing information, bibliographies, and publications on learning disabilities. It does not answer specific questions.

Center for Employment, Education & Training
College of Education
The Ohio State University
1900 Kenny Road
Columbus, OH 43210-1090
614/292-7069 or 800/848-4815 X–2-7069
Fax: 614/292-1260
E-mail: ericacve@postbox.acs.ohio_state.educ

Higher Education and Adult Training for People with Handicaps (HEATH)

One Dupont Circle, Suite 800
Washington, DC 20036
202/939-9320 or 800/544-3284

International Dyslexia Association

Chester Building
8600 LaSalle Road, Suite 382
Baltimore, MD 21286-2044
410/296-0232 or 800/222-3123
e-mail: info@interdys.org

Job Accommodation Network (JAN)

JAN provides disability-specific information on equipment and accommodations for the work place as well as a free consulting service.

West Virginia University
P. O. Box 6080
Morgantown, WV 26506-6080
800/526-7324
Fax: 304/293-5407
e-mail: jan@jan.ic.di.wvu.edu

National Center for Law and Learning Disabilities (NCLLD)

NCLLD is a non-profit education and advocacy organization providing legal information and resources for the learning disabled.

P. O. Box 368
Cabin John, MD 20818
301/469-8308

NARIC (National Rehabilitation Information Center)

8455 Colesville Road, Suite 935
Silver Spring, MD 20910-3319
800/346-2742

National Center for Learning Disabilities (NCLD)

381 Park Avenue South, Suite 1402
New York, NY 10016
212/545-7510 or 888/575-7373
Fax: 212/545-9665

Videotapes

A Leader's Guide for Youth with Learning Disabilities

A ten-minute film that shows group leaders how to include people with learning disabilities into programs using Boy Scouts as examples. Commentary by Dr. Larry Silver.

> Learning Disabilities Association of American (LDA)
> 4156 Library Road
> Pittsburgh, PA 15234-1349
> 412/341-1515 or 412/341-8077
> Fax: 412/344-6224
> Website: www.ldanatl.org

Internet Resources

Athealth.com

This online community is one of the leading providers of mental health information and services for mental health practitioners and those they serve. It consists of psychiatrists, pediatricians, family practitioners, psychologists, psychiatric nurses, social workers, counselors, researchers, educators, school psychologists, caregivers, and others who meet the diverse needs of those with mental health concerns. This is a great site to search for resources like practitioners who can provide testing and assessments.

> www.athealth.com

EASI (Equal Access to Software and Information)

Although this site is dedicated to professionals interested in access to math and science, others may find useful information on publications, technology, and internet resources for students with disabilities.

> www.rit.edu/~easi

FinAid Page

The Smart Student Guide to Financial Aid includes information on scholarships and fellowships for students with disabilities.

> www.finaid.org/documents/heath

LDOnline

This site is for anyone interested in learning disabilities. It includes articles and information as well as a celebrity quiz, artwork and a bulletin board with announcements and job postings.

www.ldonline.org/

Technology Access Center of Tucson, Inc.

This e-mail site has information on assistive technology.

tactaz@aol.com

WLDADD (Women and Learning Disabilities and ADHD)

Professionals and others interested in adult women and learning disabilities, especially those with learning differences themselves, are welcome to this listserv.

To subscribe, send the following command in the body of mail to Listserv@home.ease.lsoft.com: Subscribe WLDADD yourfirstname yourlastname."

LEARNING DISABLED STUDENTS

The Anne Ford Scholarship

The Anne Ford Scholarship is a $10,000 award given to a high school senior with an identified learning disability (LD) who is pursuing an undergraduate degree. This scholarship is offered through the National Center for Learning Disabilities (NCLD), whose mission is to increase opportunities for all individuals with learning disabilities to achieve their potential. Application can be obtained online at ncld.org. The criteria and other information are available on the website.

Applications should be sent to:
Anne Ford Scholarship
National Center for Learning Disabilities, Inc.
381 Park Avenue South, Suite 1401
New York, NY 10016-8806
212/545-7510

Fax: 212/545-9665

For further information contact: Ms. Pazit Algazi at
AFScholarship@ncld.org.

About the Author

Joy Cobb currently works as a project manager on youth-focused projects for MAXIMUS Inc. As a licensed vocational rehabilitation counselor and rehabilitation provider, Joy has managed federally funded projects that provide services for disabled and at-risk youth and adults.

Ms. Cobb graduated from The George Washington University (GWU) in Washington, DC with a BA in Psychology in 1992 and was also the recipient of the GWU Leadership Award. She received her MA from GWU in 1995 in Education and Human Development with a specialty in Vocational Rehabilitation Counseling, and was selected to be the GWU student commencement speaker.

In 1993, Ms Cobb cofounded the Professionals with Disabilities Resource Network, a clearinghouse for resources, organizations, contacts, and equipment useful for learning-disabled professionals.

Ms. Cobb is an on-call counselor at several local psychiatric treatment centers. She provides academic and vocational counseling, consulting, and accommodation assessments for the disabled in transition. As a private consultant, Ms. Cobb also presents seminars and workshops on employment issues related to the disabled in the workplace.

She is a member of Chi Sigma Iota, the national counseling honor society, and was selected for the 1995 peer presentations program. Other professional affiliations include the American Counseling Association (ACA), The Learning Disabilities Association (LDA), The Association of Rehabilitation Counselors (NARC), and The American College of Certified Forensic Counselors (ACCFC).

Ms. Cobb resides in northern Virginia with her partner, two cats and a rabbit. She is available to give presentations, workshops, seminars, and motivational speeches to students and employees. For more information, contact:

Learning How to Learn
147 North French Street
Alexandria, VA 22304
Telephone: 703/823-8348
joycobb@learninghowtolearn.org
Fax: 703/823-8349
www.learninghowtolearn.org